Savouring
IRELAND

DEDICATION
For Louis, Eva and Christine

ACKNOWLEDGEMENT
I would like to thank Christine Cullen for her generous assistance in preparing the manuscript and her helpful suggestions throughout the work. I'd also like to thank Eveleen Coyle and Fleur Robertson for the idea and for their confidence and patience, and my cooking friends and colleagues for inspiration.

EDITOR Fleur Robertson
DESIGN Louise Clements
PHOTOGRAPHY © Michael Diggin Photography
RECIPE PHOTOGRAPHY © Quadrillion Publishing Ltd
PRODUCTION Ruth Arthur, Karen Staff, Neil Randles
DIRECTOR OF PRODUCTION Graeme Proctor

Published in Ireland by
Gill & Macmillan Ltd,
Goldenbridge, Dublin 8
with associated companies throughout the world

CLB 5040

Copyright © 1998 Quadrillion Publishing Ltd
Godalming, Surrey

ISBN 0-7171-2755-9

Printed and bound in Italy

Savouring
IRELAND
Cooking through the seasons

NUALA CULLEN

GILL & MACMILLAN

contents

introduction

THE VISION of ancient Celtic Ireland that has come down to us through folklore and poetry is of a land of plenty, where poetry and music were among the important occupations of man, and honour and hospitality went hand in hand.

Through the centuries, hospitality continued to be a matter of honour, with rich and poor alike. Nearer to our own times, in the eighteenth and nineteenth centuries, successive travellers to Ireland have invariably commented on the lavish welcome, the rich variety and quantity of food and the large numbers of persons entertained. The ill-fated dependence upon the potato by almost a quarter of the population, however, and the tragic aftermath of the failure of the potato crop in the successive famines of the 1840s, is all too well known. Life changed profoundly for many people as a consequence and the tradition of prodigal hospitality was almost swept away. Ireland, however, is a natural food-producing country and, in recent decades, extensive research has given an improved understanding of the best production methods for our food resources, producing a true land of plenty, with Irish products in demand all over Europe. There has been a renaissance in Irish cooking, too. Many country-house owners have opened their homes and tables to visitors. Kitchen gardens are being restored to their former splendour, their produce forming an

important part of the cuisine. There is, too, a new generation of Irish chefs, cosmopolitan in their training though with roots in their own tradition, who are creating a discernibly Irish style of professional cooking, which allows the excellent raw materials to speak for themselves. Modern storage methods have largely made the seasons redundant, removing, to some extent, the great pleasure of looking forward to the next month's delights. In most cultures, festival days, with their attendant seasonal foods, are the only bulwark against this. We are fortunate in Ireland that many of these feasts are still observed, even if only in perfunctory way.

The recipes included in this book aim to give an idea of some of the dishes particular to the seasons, foods that have been in common use in Ireland for many hundreds of years (with one or two exceptions), though using more modern methods. I hope that you will enjoy them and that they will contribute in some measure to the enjoyment of your guests and the conviviality of the dinner table, a pleasure as important in Ireland today as it has been for centuries.

SPRING

IN NATURE'S calendar, the true new year
begins in February when the first signs
of growth appear and almost imperceptibly the
days begin to lengthen.

As the year begins to unfold, the old festive days still punctuate the seasons, many of them associated with particular foods. St Brigid has pride of place with her feast day, 1st February, appropriate for such a powerful, near-mythical figure, patroness of dairying and brewing, and in whose honour reed or rush crosses were made to be placed on house doors and cow byres. They are still made today, though more likely to be found in craft shops. St Valentine comes next and has laid claim to chocolate; and Shrove Tuesday, the day before the austerities of Lent begin, is a day when children still rush home from school to eat pancakes. St Patrick, curiously, has no particular food association, though corned beef and cabbage on this day is popular with Irish Americans. The high point of the Christian calendar is, of course, Easter, with its spiced buns and cakes – these a tradition of great antiquity – and, of course, lamb. Its sacrificial symbolism did not mar the enjoyment of those who had abstained from meat for the six weeks of Lent. Eggs, now made of chocolate, but formerly painted and decorated hen's eggs, were given as presents and used in games. After Easter, life resumes its normal tenor, the days lengthening quickly as summer approaches with its promise of early vegetables and fresher, lighter food.

SPRING
starters

MUSSELS WITH BACON
AND RED WINE

'Lord Smart (to Neverout): Tom, they say fish should swim thrice.
Neverout: How is that, my Lord?
Lord Smart: Why, Tom, first it should swim in the Sea (Do you mind me?), then it should swim
in Butter; and at last Sirrah, it should swim in good Claret.'
Jonathan Swift, *Polite Conversation*

3¹/₂ pints/2 litres live mussels
6 streaky bacon rashers
8 fl oz/225 ml red wine
2 tablespoons butter
1 fresh thyme sprig
4 shallots
2 garlic cloves, finely chopped
3 large ripe tomatoes,
   de-seeded and chopped
1 tablespoon plain flour
2 tablespoons chopped
   fresh parsley
salt and freshly ground
   black pepper

Clean the mussels thoroughly, discarding any that are broken or don't close when sharply tapped, and put them in a large saucepan, with the wine. Cover, bring to the boil and cook for 2 minutes, shaking the pan from time to time, until the mussels are open. Remove the mussels to a bowl, discarding any that do not open. Strain the liquid carefully into a bowl, discarding any sand or grit.

Melt 1 tablespoon of butter in a saucepan, add the thyme and bacon and cook until crisp. Then add the shallots and garlic and cook until soft. Add the tomatoes. Mash the remaining butter and the flour together and stir into the saucepan, a piece at a time, stirring until the flour is cooked and the sauce is smooth. Add the mussel liquid gradually, stirring until the sauce has thickened. If it is too thick, add a little water. Reheat the mussels in the sauce for a few moments and stir in the parsley. Check and adjust the seasoning. Serve with fresh crusty bread.

Serves 6, as a starter

Ruined village, Blasket Islands
Previous page: Co. Kerry smallholding

SPRING GREEN SOUP

Soups of this type were very popular in the past, providing much needed vitamins and minerals after a winter diet of dried pulses and winter roots. The ingredients can be varied according to which shoots have made their appearance or are available in shops.

large handful of sorrel leaves
large handful of spinach
handful of young nettles or
   dandelion leaves
heart of a small green cabbage
2 oz/55 g butter
2 onions, finely chopped
2 garlic cloves, chopped
chopped fresh thyme
2 potatoes, peeled and
   chopped
1³/₄ pint/1 litre chicken stock,
or milk and water
¹/₄ pint/150 ml cream
salt and freshly ground
   black pepper

Wash all the leaves thoroughly in salted water, removing any coarse stalks or ribs. Keep the nettles separate. Prepare the cabbage in the same way, shake dry and finely chop.

Melt the butter in a large saucepan and gently sweat the onions, garlic, spinach, cabbage, sorrel and thyme. Add the potatoes and the stock, or milk and water, and simmer until the potato is soft. Then add the nettles and cook until they are tender, about 30 minutes. Liquidise, add the cream, adjust the seasoning and serve.

Serves 6

SPICY CARROT SOUP

4–5 large carrots, grated
1 tablespoon oil
1 tablespoon mustard seeds
1 oz/30 g butter
2 medium onions, chopped
1 tablespoon coriander seeds
2 pints/1.2 litres chicken or
   vegetable stock
2 tablespoons porridge oats
3 teaspoons cider vinegar
juice and grated zest of a
   large orange
salt and freshly ground
   black pepper
chopped fresh coriander, to
   garnish (optional)
cream, to garnish (optional)

Heat the oil in a large saucepan and add the mustard seeds, heating until they pop. Add the butter and onions and cook on a low heat until they begin to soften. Then add the carrots and coriander seeds and continue cooking for 5–6 minutes. Add half the stock and the porridge oats and cook a further few minutes. If you like a smooth soup, purée the mixture at this point. Return to the saucepan, add the vinegar, orange juice and zest and remaining stock. Season well, simmer for a few moments and serve.

The soup can be garnished with a swirl of cream and some chopped, fresh coriander if you so wish.

Serves 6

Spring vegetable garden

SOUSED HERRINGS

The herring has been a staple of the Irish diet for centuries and its seasonal appearance was greeted with pleasure by rich and poor alike. Huge fleets set out from Killybegs in Donegal in search of the 'silver darlin's'. Originally, sousing was a simple method of preserving surplus herring or mackerel, but it became a popular dish in its own right. The sousing liquid here is a mild version and, if the herrings are to be eaten hot, leave them in the marinade for several hours, or overnight, to allow the flavour to develop. For a spicier flavour, add a little chilli.

8–10 herring fillets
8–10 shallots
2–3 bay leaves
1 onion, sliced

FOR THE MARINADE
¹/₂ pint/280 ml cider or
   white-wine vinegar
¹/₂ pint/280 ml dry cider or
   white wine
2 teaspoons juniper berries,
   slightly crushed
chilli powder or chopped
   fresh chillies, to taste
1-2 tablespoons each of
   brown sugar, mustard seeds
   and black peppercorns

Boil the marinade ingredients together gently for a few minutes. Cool and allow to infuse for 30 minutes. Preheat the oven to 150°C/300°F/Gas Mark 2. Lay out the fish fillets on a board and arrange a peeled shallot and a piece of bay leaf on each half. Roll up and secure with a cocktail stick. Arrange in an ovenproof dish, strew the onion slices over the top and pour the marinade into the dish. Cover with foil and bake for 30–40 minutes.

Cool before packing into a plastic box, which will allow the cooking liquid to cover them, and chill, overnight if possible. The herrings can be kept for 2–3 days in the refrigerator.

OYSTERS WITH SPICY PORK PATTIES

St Valentine's Day calls for something special: delicious, of course, with amorous associations, and not too much trouble. The old fashion of eating chilled oysters and chipolatas (tiny hot spicy sausages) with champagne or white wine seems ideal. Chipolatas may be hard to find so prepare and chill your own pork patties the day before and then cook them quickly, for 10 minutes or so, when required. Serve hot, alternating with the chilled oysters.

12 oysters, opened (see
   below), on the deep half of
   the shell
12 oz/340 g lean pork, finely
   minced
¹/₂ onion, finely chopped
1 garlic clove
1 oz/30 g butter
2 teaspoons Yorkshire relish or
   Worcestershire sauce
a pinch each of dried thyme,
   grated nutmeg and hot
   chilli powder
1 tablespoon finely chopped
   fresh parsley

Cook the onion and garlic in a little butter, until soft. Chill before mixing with the pork, if the patties are being prepared in advance. Mix the meat with the remaining butter, relish or sauce, seasonings and herbs and stir in the onion and garlic. Mix thoroughly and, with floured hands, shape into small patties, about 1¹/₂ inches/2 cm wide. They should be hot and spicy but not so they kill the taste of the oysters and wine. Cook them in a frying pan, without any extra fat, for about 10 minutes.

Note: to open an oyster, hold it firmly in your left hand and insert a short, sharp knife near the hinge, working it from right to left until it begins to release; then prise it open.

Serves 2

COD'S ROE AND COD'S ROE PÂTÉ

The season for cod's roe is very short, a mere 2–3 weeks between February and March, so it is important to make the most of it and, as the roes freeze well, either raw or cooked, it's a good idea to buy extra when they are available. Smaller roes are more delicate in texture but the larger ones are very good, too.

To cook, simply tie the roe loosely in a plastic bag, cover with boiling water and simmer slowly until it is firm to the touch. Leave to cool and remove from the bag. The simplest and most traditional preparation is to cut it into thick slices, dip in seasoned flour, or egg and breadcrumbs, and fry gently in a mixture of butter and oil, until crisp. Serve for breakfast, with crisp bacon and grilled tomatoes or mushrooms, or for lunch with creamy mashed potato and a slice of lemon.

**4–5 oz/110–140 g cooked
   cod's roe
2–3 oz/55–75 g butter, melted
juice and grated zest of
   $^1/_2$ lemon
salt
cayenne or chilli pepper
   to taste
fresh chives, chopped**

Purée all the ingredients in a food processor, until smooth. Pack into little ramekins and chill. This is delicious with hot toast, as a starter.
Serves 4, as a starter

Donkey plough, Co. Kerry

POTATO SOUP WITH SALMON AND CHIVES

This rather different potato soup uses the excellent farmed salmon that is available all year round.

6 medium potatoes, peeled
   and chopped
6 oz/170 g salmon, cutlet or
   tail piece
2 tablespoons finely chopped
   fresh chives
2 oz/55 g butter
1 onion, finely chopped
2 leeks, chopped
1 bay leaf
1 pint/575 ml chicken or
   fish stock
1 pint/575 ml milk
salt and freshly ground
   black pepper

Put the salmon in a small saucepan, just barely cover with water, and poach gently until the fish is cooked, about 10 minutes. Remove from the water, skin, remove bones and flake. Add the water to the stock.

Melt the butter in a large saucepan and cook the onion and leeks until tender but not coloured. Add the potatoes, bay leaf, seasoning and the stock, and cook until the potatoes are soft. Then purée in a food processor, first removing the bay leaf. Return to the saucepan. Next add the milk, chives, and salmon and gently bring to the boil. Adjust the seasoning and serve hot, with brown scones, buttered.

Serves 6

S P R I N G
m a i n   c o u r s e s

HAKE BAKED IN PAPER

This method of cooking was widely used in the past to protect delicate morsels from the heat of the open fire. Baking parchment is the ideal material, sealing in the flavours and appearing somehow more aesthetic on the plate than foil. The fish can be served with a selection of roasted vegetables.

4 hake fillets, weighing
  4–8 oz/110–225 g each
2 oz/55 g butter
1 large red pepper
chopped fresh dill or
  marjoram, leave some
  for garnishing
4 tablespoons dry vermouth
  or white wine
8–10 live mussels, to
  garnish
salt and freshly ground
  black pepper

Preheat the oven to 180°C/350°F/Gas Mark 4. Cut 4 pieces of parchment large enough to enclose the pieces of fish. Season and butter the fish well and place one on each piece of parchment. Slice the pepper into thin rounds, removing any seeds or white membrane and place one or two slices on top of each piece of fish. Sprinkle a pinch of chopped dill or marjoram on each and pour on a tablespoon of vermouth or wine. Bring the 2 sides of the paper together and pleat lengthways, tucking the ends firmly under the packet to seal. Place the parcels in a baking dish, brush with butter and bake for about 20–25 minutes, depending on the thickness of the fillets.

Steam the mussels open in a covered pan with a few tablespoons of water. Discard any that don't open. When the fish is ready, cut a slit in the paper with scissors, garnish with the mussels and herbs and serve. It is usual to allow each guest to open their own parcel but experience suggests that it is better to make the initial incision first.

Serves 4

Tralee Bay, Co. Kerry

SALMON CAKES WITH DILL SAUCE

*To make these fish cakes, use either a tail piece or cutlets or, better still, the
buttery remains of a whole salmon.*

1¹/₂ lb/675 g salmon
3 tablespoons finely
   chopped shallot
1 egg yolk
1 tablespoon lemon juice
3 oz/75 g butter, melted
1 tablespoon finely chopped
   fresh herbs
5 oz/140 g breadcrumbs
1 tablespoon cream, if
   necessary
1 egg, beaten
2 tablespoons each wholemeal
flour and breadcrumbs, mixed
salt and freshly ground
   black pepper
oil and butter, for frying

FOR THE DILL SAUCE
8 fl oz/225 ml hot milk
1 tablespoon butter

1 tablespoon plain flour
3–4 tablespoons crème fraîche
2 tablespoons finely chopped
fresh dill or 2 teaspoons
   dried dill
salt and freshly ground black
   pepper

Poach the salmon in salted water
for 12–15 minutes. Remove any
skin and bones and flake the fish.
Sauté the shallot in a little of the
butter, until softened. Mix the
salmon, shallot, egg yolk, lemon
juice, melted butter, herbs and
seasoning together. Add the
breadcrumbs and work well
together. Add a spoonful of cream
if the mixture is too dry. Firmly
shape into 4 or 8 cakes, with
floured hands, and then dip into

the beaten egg and then into the
breadcrumb and flour mixture.
Melt a little butter and oil in a large
frying-pan and cook for 5–6
minutes on each side, until crisp
and very hot. Drain on kitchen
paper and serve with the dill
sauce.

   To make the sauce, melt the
butter in a saucepan, whisk in the
flour and stir until cooked, about a
minute. Off the heat, gradually
whisk in the hot milk. Bring back to
the boil and stir until the sauce
thickens. Add the crème fraîche
and dill and season to taste.

   *Serves 4 as a main course, or 8
as a first course*

Lough Carra, Co. Mayo

BUTTER BEAN
HOT POT

*This comforting dish is an
example of the homely cooking
we all love to return to.*

**8 oz/225 g butter beans,
  soaked overnight
1 lb/450 g piece of bacon,
streaky or collar cut, cubed
  oil, for frying
1 lb/450 g potatoes, sliced
1 lb/450 g onions, sliced
1 lb/450 g sharp cooking
  apples, peeled and sliced
chopped fresh thyme
1 or 2 fresh sage leaves
$^1/_2$ pint/225 ml stock
  or water
salt and freshly ground
  black pepper**

Drain the beans, change the water,
bring to the boil and boil for 10
minutes; then simmer until almost
soft but not breaking up, about 40
minutes.

  Preheat the oven to
150°C/300°F/Gas Mark 2. Brown
the meat in a little oil in a heavy
pan. Remove the meat and then
brown the onions in the same pan.
Layer the onions, bacon, apples,
beans and potatoes in a greased,
ovenproof casserole, sprinkling
with pepper and thyme and
tucking in the sage leaves. Finish
with a layer of potatoes. Add a
very little salt and pour the stock
over all. Cover with foil, or a lid,
and bake for about 2 hours.

  Remove the foil and continue
cooking until the potatoes are
brown. Add a little more stock, if
necessary. A simple green salad is
good with this.

Serves 4

CHICKEN AND CHEESE
WRAPPED IN BACON

This simple dish uses the traditionally popular combination of chicken and ham, with the piquant addition of Cashel Blue, one of Ireland's finest cheeses, which gives just the right note of acidity to the dish.

**4 boneless, skinless
  chicken breasts
8 rindless streaky bacon
  rashers
6 oz/170 g Cashel Blue cheese
2–3 fresh sage leaves, torn
grated lemon zest
1 oz/30 g butter
a glass of white wine,
  vermouth or chicken stock
2–3 tablespoons cream
salt and freshly ground
  black pepper**

**TO GARNISH
lemon wedges
fresh sage leaves**

Place a chicken breast flat on a board and, with a sharp knife, slice in two horizontally. Cover each piece with cling film and beat gently with a rolling pin until slightly larger. Cut each bacon rasher in two and stretch them out by stroking with the blade of a large knife. Lay two pieces of bacon side by side on the board, put a tiny piece of sage on top and cover with a piece of chicken. Season the chicken well and add some lemon zest. Cut the cheese into eight fingers and place one on the piece of chicken, roll up the bacon and chicken and secure with cocktail sticks or thread. Continue with the rest of the bacon and chicken until you have 8 rolls.

In a heavy pan, brown the rolls in the butter, turning frequently, for about 10 minutes, until the chicken appears cooked and the cheese is beginning to melt. Remove the rolls to a hot dish and remove the cocktail sticks. Add the wine, vermouth or stock to the pan, scraping up all the sediment, and bubbling well for a few moments to reduce the wine. Add the cream, bubble again for 2–3 minutes, and then check and adjust the seasoning. Pour a little sauce on to each plate and arrange the rolls on top.

Garnish with lemon wedges and a few sage leaves. Serve with a crisp salad or a green vegetable.
Serves 4

LAMB'S LETTUCE AND DANDELION LEAF SALAD

Dandelions are thought to have great curative powers: whether this is true, or not, they make an excellent salad.

8 oz/225 g lamb's lettuce
8 oz/225 g young
  dandelion leaves
3 tablespoons wine or
  cider vinegar
6 strips of streaky bacon
1 garlic clove
2–3 oz/55–75 g Cashel
  Blue cheese
salt and freshly ground
  black pepper

FOR THE VINAIGRETTE
1 teaspoon french mustard
1 tablespoon cider or
  wine vinegar
4–5 tablespoons olive oil
salt and freshly ground
  black pepper

Wash the lamb's lettuce and set aside to drain. Wash the dandelion leaves and trim the stalks. Dry well and put them in the salad bowl.

Heat the vinegar and pour it over the dandelion leaves; toss and leave for about 15 minutes. This helps to soften them. Pour off any surplus vinegar.

Meanwhile, make the vinaigrette by mixing the mustard, vinegar and salt and pepper together well. Whisk in the oil, until smooth.

Fry the bacon in its own fat, with the garlic, until crisp. Remove the garlic and pour the bacon and pan juices over the dandelions. Add the lamb's lettuce to the bowl and toss well with a little vinaigrette. Season to taste. Crumble the cheese on top and serve while the bacon is still warm. For a first course, arrange the salad on individual plates.

Serves 6

FRICASSÉE OF PORK

2 lb/900 g boneless
   pork, cubed
1 large onion, chopped
1 oz/30 g butter
1 tablespoon oil
12 oz/340 g button
   mushrooms
1 tablespoon plain flour
2 teaspoons ground cumin
$^1/_4$ pint/150 ml dry white
   wine or stock
$^1/_2$ pint/280 ml cream
2 celery sticks, thinly sliced
salt and freshly ground
   black pepper

Preheat the oven to
150°C/300°F/Gas Mark 2. Soften
the onion in half the butter and oil;
then transfer to an ovenproof dish.
Add the mushrooms to the pan

and cook for a few minutes, until
lightly browned. Pour, with any
juice, into the dish. Toss the cubed
pork in the flour and cumin and
brown in the pan with the
remaining oil and butter. Add to
the dish. Sprinkle any remaining
flour into the pan and stir for a few
moments to cook. Add the wine
or stock, scraping up all the
sediment thoroughly. Now add the
cream, check and adjust the
seasoning and stir well. Pour over
the pork mixture, stir in the sliced
celery, cover and cook gently until
the pork is tender, 45–60 minutes.
Serve with creamy mashed
potatoes or rice.

   Serves 6

Lazy beds in Ventry on the Dingle Peninsula

SPRING LAMB CUTLETS IN PASTRY

Easter is the time of renewal and the lamb symbolises the return of life in many cultures. Roast baby lamb is traditionally served for Easter Sunday dinner and nothing is more delicious, especially when it is moist and tender and delicately pink. As a change from the usual leg of lamb, try this rack of lamb in pastry, a great party dish and very easy to carve – simply cut down between the cutlet bones. You will need 2 cutlets per person, possibly 3 if they are very tiny. This sauce is the invariable sauce for lamb in Ireland and it is very much an eighteenth-century concept; the vinegar was thought to counteract the fattiness of the meat.

1 rack of lamb (about 8 cutlets)
1 lb/450 g puff pastry
2 oz/55 g butter
4 shallots, finely chopped
8 oz/225 g mushrooms, finely chopped
4 oz/110 g dried apricots, finely chopped
1 egg, beaten, to glaze
chopped fresh mint or oregano
grated lemon zest and juice
salt and freshly ground black pepper

FOR THE MINT SAUCE
1–2 tablespoons chopped fresh mint
1–2 tablespoons sugar, or to taste
1–2 tablespoons cider or white wine vinegar
3–4 tablespoons water

Preheat the oven to 220°C/425°F/Gas Mark 7. Rub the lamb with half the butter and season well. Roast the meat for 8-10 minutes. Allow to cool completely.

Gently cook the shallots, mushrooms, apricots and mint or oregano in the remaining butter until the juices have thickened. Season this well with lemon zest and a little lemon juice and plenty of black pepper. Press the stuffing between the cutlets. Roll out the pastry into a sheet large enough to enclose the rack and fold around the meat, allowing the bones to protrude. Cover these with foil, to prevent them from burning.

Decorate with pastry trimmings. Wash over the pastry with the beaten egg. Heat the oven to 180°C/350°F/Gas Mark 4 and bake until the pastry is browned, about 25-30 minutes. Serve with mint sauce.

To make the sauce, bring all the ingredients to the boil; then remove from the heat, stirring to dissolve the sugar. Allow to cool. More or less mint can be used and apple jelly can be used instead of the sugar.
Serves 4

CORNED BEEF AND CABBAGE

*'Corned' beef, an old word for pickled beef, can be
prepared at home using the method for Spiced Beef
(see page 118), leaving out the spices.*

**3–4 lb/1.4–1.8 kg tail end or
  silverside of beef**
1 green or savoy cabbage
2 carrots
2 celery sticks
1 onion
1 tablespoon brown sugar
1 tablespoon mustard powder
2–3 cloves

Prepare the beef as for Spiced
Beef (see page 118) and leave to
pickle for 10 days. If you are buying
shop-pickled beef, soak the meat
for several hours in cold water.

Put the vegetables and
seasonings, except the cabbage,
into a large saucepan. Cover with
cold water and bring it to the boil
very slowly. Simmer gently for
about 2 hours (20 minutes per
lb/450 g). When the meat is
tender, turn off the heat and rest it
in the water for 30 minutes, while
you prepare the cabbage.

Wash and quarter the cabbage.
Pour a ladleful of the cooking
water from the meat and enough
boiling water to fill a saucepan to
half the depth of the cabbage. Add
the cabbage and boil hard, without
a lid, until the cabbage is just
tender. Slice the beef and arrange
on a deep dish with the cabbage
around it.

The traditional method is to put
the cabbage into the pot with the
meat for the last 15 minutes
cooking time, but I feel the rather
lean meat benefits from a resting
period and the cabbage is less
greasy when cooked on its own.
Serve with mustard and plain
boiled potatoes.

Serves 6–8

IRISH STEW

*There is much argument concerning the authentic Irish stew,
but for most of us, I suspect, the 'authentic' dish is the one made in
our own families. The pure tradition uses only mutton,
potatoes, onion and seasoning, and this, I think, is generally agreed to
be the thing. Some contemporary recipes include carrots, and even
celery, so you can make your own choice.*

**2 lb/900 g neck of lamb
  chops**
1 lb/450 g onions
2¹/₂ lb/1.15 kg potatoes
1 oz/30 g butter
2 carrots, chopped
2 celery sticks, chopped
1 large fresh thyme sprig
**³/₄ pint/425 ml water or lamb
  stock**
white pepper and salt

Chop the onions coarsely. Peel and
slice the potatoes thickly. Season
the chops well. Put the butter in
the bottom of a heavy saucepan
and then layer the meat and
vegetables, finishing with a layer of
potatoes. Bury the thyme in the
centre. Pour in the stock or water.

Cover the pan tightly with foil and
a lid, bring to the boil and then
immediately lower the heat and
cook gently on the lowest possible
heat for about 1¹/₂ hours. The meat
and vegetables should cook in
their juices with very little liquid
left at the end, so watch for
burning. It may be necessary to
add more liquid.

Serves 6

Ironmongers, Bunratty Folk Park, Co. Clare

SPRING
desserts

IRISH CURD TART

*The ancient poetry of Gaelic Ireland has many images of feasting on
rich curds, and sweet milk-foods are still enjoyed today.*

1 lb/450 g cottage cheese
juice and grated zest of
  1 lemon
2 tablespoons caster sugar,
  plus a little extra
2 oz/55 g ground almonds
4 eggs
2 tablespoons raisins
grated nutmeg

FOR THE PASTRY
3 oz/75 g butter
5 oz/140 g flour
1 tablespoon caster sugar
1 egg yolk, beaten
1–2 tablespoons very cold
  water

Make the pastry in the usual way,
rubbing the butter into the flour
and sugar and moistening with the
egg yolk and 1 or 2 tablespoons of
water, as required. Roll out to fit a
greased 8 inch/20 cm tart tin and
chill for 30 minutes.

Preheat the oven to
180°C/350°F/ Gas Mark 4. Blend
or sieve the cottage cheese, lemon
zest, sugar and ground almonds.
Sharpen to taste, by adding a little
lemon juice. Beat the eggs
together, and then fold thoroughly,
with the raisins, into the cheese
mixture. Pour into the prepared
pastry case and sprinkle a little
sugar and grated nutmeg over the
top. Bake for 30–40 minutes until
golden brown. The mixture will
gently subside as it cools.

Serve warm or cold. A little
whipped cream is good with it, if
it's to be served warm.

The raisins can be soaked in a
spoonful of whiskey for a few
hours first, to plump them up and
give a little extra flavour.

Serves 6

SIMNEL CAKE

4 oz/110 g butter
3 oz/75 g brown sugar
2 tablespoons golden syrup
4 large eggs
9 oz/250 g self-raising flour
1 teaspoon each ground
cinnamon, grated nutmeg and
  ground ginger
12 oz/340 g mixed dried fruit
4 oz/110 g candied peel
1 tablespoon apricot jam,
  warmed

FOR THE MARZIPAN
1 lb/450 g ground almonds
8 oz/225 g caster sugar
8 oz/225 g icing sugar
2 eggs
1 dessertspoon lemon juice
1 teaspoon almond essence

To make the marzipan, sift the almonds with the sugars. Beat the eggs, lemon juice and the flavouring together and stir into the almond mixture, kneading well until a smooth paste is formed. Break off eleven walnut-sized pieces, roll into balls and set aside (these were said to represent the twelve apostles of Jesus, minus Judas). Divide the remaining piece in two and roll into two rounds that will fit the cake tin.

To make the cake, preheat the oven to 170°C/325°F/Gas Mark 3 and grease and line an 8 inch/20 cm cake tin, approx. 3 inch/8 cm deep. Cream the butter, sugar and syrup together. Add the eggs, beating well after each addition. Sift the flour and spices together and fold into the mixture thoroughly. Fold in the fruit and peel.

Place half the mixture in the prepared tin and gently cover with a layer of marzipan. Put the remainder of the mixture on top. Bake for one hour, then cover with a piece of foil and reduce the heat to 150°C/300°F/Gas Mark 2 and cook for a further half hour. Test with a skewer, which should come out clean; remember not to push it down into the marzipan layer.

When cooked, remove to a wire rack. Remove from the tin and continue cooling.

When the cake is firm, after about half an hour, spread the apricot jam on top and press the second marzipan round on top, knocking up the edge decoratively. Put the cake under the grill, not too close to the heat, for a few moments to toast the top. Watch carefully as it burns quickly. Now dampen the marzipan balls and press them around the top of the cake. Lower the grill rack and return the cake to the grill, to toast the balls.

A yellow ribbon can be tied around the cake, for a festive appearance.

Tim Healy Pass, Co. Cork

ORANGE CREAMS

Seville oranges, both zest and pith, were used to make these delicious creams in the past, when oranges were a seasonal commodity. One Seville orange, with its stronger flavour, would be sufficient.

2 oranges
4 egg yolks
2 egg whites
¹/₂ pint/280 ml cream and milk mixed
about 2 tablespoons caster sugar
1 tablespoon brandy, rum or orange liqueur
whipped cream, to serve

Choose unwaxed oranges, if possible. Scrub the skins well and then with a potato peeler, peel the zest off, not too thinly (a little pith will give more flavour). Squeeze the juice. Put the orange zest, with the juice and a little extra water into a small saucepan and simmer very gently until the zest is soft. This takes a surprisingly long time, perhaps 45 minutes, and you will probably need to add a few spoonfuls of water from time to time. When the zest is soft, allow the liquid to evaporate, being careful it doesn't burn.

Preheat the oven to 150°C/300°F/Gas Mark 2. Purée the zest in a mini processor or a mortar and pestle. Add the eggs, cream and milk, sugar to taste and the brandy, rum or liqueur and pour into 4 buttered ramekins. A strip of peel or a small, skinned orange section can be gently laid on top of each. Set the ramekins in water in a roasting tin and bake for about 45 minutes, until set when tested with a knife. Serve cold, in the ramekins, with a spoonful of whipped cream on top.

Serves 4

PANCAKES

These are traditionally eaten on Shrove Tuesday, the day before Lent begins. Shrove Tuesday pancakes are served in the simplest manner, with sugar, lemon juice and butter and it is hard to improve on this. However, for a simple and delicious dessert, fill them with Cinnamon Custard (see page 37).

8 oz/225 g plain flour
1 tablespoon caster sugar
a pinch of ground ginger or grated nutmeg
2 eggs, beaten
2 oz/55 g butter, melted
1 pint/575 ml milk
oil and melted butter, for frying

Mix the dry ingredients together and then add the eggs, butter and milk. Beat thoroughly and leave for at least an hour for the flour to expand.

Heat a heavy 7 inch/18 cm frying-pan until hot and add a teaspoon each of oil and butter. Swirl around the pan and pour the surplus into a little dish. Pour a small ladleful of batter into the pan and swirl around, to form a thin skin. Cook until golden brown; then turn with a palette knife and cook for a few moments longer. (The first couple of pancakes invariably break up or stick.) Dip a pastry brush in oil and melted butter and brush the pan again before cooking each pancake. Stack, with greaseproof paper between each pancake. They can be reheated gently in the oven or microwave.

Serves 4

The Skelligs from Puffin Island

CHOCOLATE CAKE WITH MOCCA FILLING

This delicious chocolate cake is suitable either for a luxurious afternoon tea or a dinner party dessert to celebrate St Valentine's Day.

FOR THE CAKE
8 oz/225 g plain flour
3 oz/75 g cocoa powder
4 large eggs, separated
5 tablespoons sunflower oil
**8 oz/225 g golden
   granulated sugar**

FOR THE FILLING
3 oz/75 g butter
4 oz/110 g icing sugar, sifted
**2 teaspoons instant coffee,
dissolved in 1 tablespoon
   hot water**
1 tablespoon rum

TO DECORATE
³/₄ pint/425 ml cream
1 tablespoon caster sugar
**6 oz/170 g good dark
   chocolate**

Preheat the oven to 190°C/375°F/Gas Mark 5 and grease and line an 8 inch/20 cm cake tin.

Sieve the flour and cocoa together. Beat the egg yolks, oil and sugar together, until pale and creamy. Fold in the flour and cocoa. Beat the egg whites to a soft, dropping consistency and fold carefully into the flour mixture. Pour into the prepared tin, making a depression in the centre. Bake for about 45 minutes. Test the cake with a skewer; if it comes out clean, the cake is cooked.

Cool the cake in the tin for 10 minutes before turning it on to a cake rack. When cold, split the cake in half horizontally.

To make the filling, beat the butter to a cream with the icing sugar, beat in the coffee solution and rum. Spread lavishly on the bottom layer and put the cake together. Any surplus filling can go on the top of the cake.

Whip the cream with the caster sugar, until soft. Reserving some for decoration, cover the entire cake. With a potato peeler, pare some large flakes of chocolate for the top of the cake; then grate the remainder. Cover the sides of the cake with the grated chocolate, using a palette knife. Pipe or spoon the reserved cream around the top and scatter the chocolate flakes in the centre.

Serves 8

Hag's Glen, McGillicuddy's Reeks, Co. Kerry

CINNAMON CUSTARD

This is an ideal filling for pancakes (see page 35) and it also makes a wonderful filling for a sponge cake.

17 fl oz/500 ml milk
1 teaspoon grated lemon zest
¹/₂ cinnamon stick
4 oz/110 g caster sugar
2 oz/55 g cornflour
1 vanilla pod
4 egg yolks

Mix the egg yolks with the sugar and cornflour.

Bring the milk to the boil slowly, with the cinnamon stick and vanilla pod, cover and leave to infuse for 15 minutes.

Remove the cinnamon and vanilla. Bring the milk back to the boil and pour on to the egg mixture, stirring rapidly. Return the mixture to the saucepan, over a low heat, and stir continually until the mixture thickens slightly. Do not allow to boil or the eggs will scramble. Pour into a shallow bowl, to cool.

To serve, fill the pancakes with a few spoonfuls of the custard and sprinkle with a few drops of brandy. Reheat in a moderate oven (180°C/350°F/Gas Mark 4), for 15 minutes.

Serves 4

SPRING
baking

RHUBARB CREAM WITH
GINGER BISCUITS

*Creams such as this are to be found in family recipe
books of the eighteenth century and are the forerunners of the fruit
'fools' of today. Ginger biscuits contrast well
with the creamy rhubarb.*

1½ lb/675 g rhubarb, washed
   and trimmed
4 eggs
2 oz/55 g caster sugar
1 tablespoon grated lemon
   zest
4 oz/125 ml cream
2 tablespoons golden
   granulated sugar

TO GARNISH
strawberries, sliced if large
fresh lemon balm or mint
   leaves

Preheat the oven to
170°C/325°F/Gas Mark 3. Chop
the rhubarb and cook gently,
without water, until the juice runs
and the rhubarb is tender (the
microwave is ideal for this). Pour
off any excess juice and beat the
rhubarb to a purée with a fork.
Beat the eggs with the sugar in a
small bowl. Bring the cream to a
boil and pour on to the eggs,
stirring well. Pour the egg mixture
into the rhubarb, add the lemon
zest and mix well. Put the mixture
into a 2 pint/1.2 litre ovenproof
dish. Sprinkle the top with the
brown sugar. Stand this in another
larger dish filled with water and
bake for about 45 minutes.

Remove from the oven and chill.
   The cream can be served from
the dish or put in glasses and
garnished with strawberries and
mint or lemon balm leaves.
   Serves 4–5

GINGER BISCUITS
8 oz/225 g self-raising flour
¼ teaspoon salt
1 teaspoon ground ginger, or
   to taste
4 oz/110 g butter
4 oz/110 g light brown sugar
3–4 tablespoons milk

Preheat the oven to
170°C/325°F/Gas Mark 3. Sift the
flour, salt and ginger together.
Cream the butter and sugar, fold in
the flour and mix to a pliable
dough, adding milk as required.
Break off walnut-sized pieces of
dough and roll into balls. Place
these on parchment-lined trays
and press out slightly with the back
of a fork dipped in flour. Space out
somewhat, as they will spread.
Bake for 10–12 minutes.
   Remove to a wire rack with a
palette knife. They will keep well in
an airtight tin.
   Makes about 30

Blasket Island, Co. Kerry

Spring

HOT CROSS BUNS

Hot cross buns are synonymous with Easter, though, in fact, they are now thought to predate Christianity. Whatever their origins, they are delicious, especially toasted with plenty of butter. They are incomparably better home-made and, with dried yeast, very easy to make.

1¹/₂ lb/675 g plain flour

¹/₂ oz/15 g sachet of easy-
   blend dried yeast

2 teaspoons sugar

1 teaspoon salt

3 teaspoons ground mixed
   spice, or to taste

2 oz/55 g butter

¹/₂ pint/280 ml warm milk

1 large egg, beaten

5 oz/140 g mixed dried fruit

2 oz/55 g candied peel

4 oz/110 g sugar and ¹/₂ pint/
   280 ml water, boiled
   together to form a syrup

Mix the flour, dried yeast, sugar, salt and mixed spice together. Soften the butter in the warm milk and add the beaten egg.

Make a well in the flour and pour in the liquid, drawing in the flour from the sides and kneading well until a pliable dough has formed (this can be done in a food processor). Knead in the fruit and peel. Cover the dough with cling film and allow to rise until doubled in bulk.

Knock down the dough and knead again for a few moments. Then divide into 12–14 pieces and shape into balls. Arrange them on oiled baking trays and allow them to rise for a further 20–30 minutes. Mix 2 tablespoons of flour and 1 tablespoon of water together and trail a cross on the top of each bun. Preheat the oven to 190°C/375°F/Gas Mark 5. Bake for about 20 minutes (they will sound hollow when tapped underneath).

With a pastry brush, paint the buns with the syrup and return to the oven for 5 minutes, to set. Cool on a wire rack

WHOLEMEAL SCONES

14 oz/400 g coarse
   wholemeal flour

6 oz/170 g plain white flour

¹/₂ teaspoon salt

3 teaspoons baking powder

2 oz/55 g brown sugar

3 oz/75 g butter

2 eggs

8 fl oz/225 ml milk

Preheat the oven to 220°C/425°F/Gas Mark 7. Sieve the salt and baking powder with the white flour and mix thoroughly with the wholemeal flour. Add the sugar and rub in the butter with your fingers. Beat the eggs and milk together. Reserve a tablespoon or so, and fold the rest quickly and lightly into the flour. Add a little more milk, if necessary, to form a relaxed dough. Roll out on a floured surface to 1 inch/2.5 cm thick and cut into 12 rounds or squares. Brush the tops with the reserved milk/egg mixture. Bake for about 20 minutes, or until there is a hollow sound when the scones are tapped underneath. Cool on a wire rack.

Country chickens. Overleaf: Coumhoola Valley, Co. Cork

SUMMER

MAY, I think is the most exciting
month in the garden. Suddenly everything
is coming into bloom and, for the cook,
early herbs are abundant.

Sorrel, for wonderful sauces, is ready and waiting for the salmon to become plentiful. In June, thoughts turn to outdoor eating, for many of us one of life's great pleasures though, given the variable Irish climate, picnics in the country or seaside often turn out to be, to quote Dr Johnson on another subject, 'a triumph of hope over experience'. All serious picnickers are undeterred by this and indeed some of my happiest recollections involve eating in a downpour, the taste of rain in the wine.

The west of Ireland is the place to be on Midsummer's Night, where the sunset lingers until midnight, and driving through the countryside at night on St John's Eve, 23rd June, bonfires can still be seen on the hills, echoes of a ritual older than Christianity.

Ritual brings the summer to a close with the feast of *Lúnasa*, the last Sunday of July, when the custom of picking *fraughauns* (bilberries) still lingers, and was, in fact, the occasion of one of my most memorable rained-out picnics. Perhaps our levity had displeased Crom Dubh, the ancient god of darkness whose feast day this is, and who was said to place his curse on *fraughans* picked after 1st August.

SUMMER
starters

POTTED SALMON

This eighteenth-century Irish recipe uses ginger, mace, lemon zest and bay leaves. There are no exact measurements. The spices can be adjusted to taste and the quantity of fish available, but the initial salting should be generous. This is delicious with toast as a first course or as part of a buffet. The salmon can be potted in individual ramekins, if you prefer.

1 lb/450 g salmon
2 tablespoons sea salt
1 teaspoon ground mace
grated zest of 1 lemon
1 bay leaf
a pinch of ground ginger
4 oz/110 g butter, clarified
  (see below)

Preheat the oven to 150°C/300°F/Gas Mark 2. Skin and remove the bones from the fish and then cut it into pieces. Rub all the surfaces well with salt and leave for 3 hours.

Scrape the salt from the fish, wipe with kitchen paper but don't wash it. Pack the fish into an earthenware or Pyrex dish, with the mace, lemon zest and the bay leaf, and cover with foil. Bake for about 30 minutes, or until the fish is cooked.

Pour off the juices and remove the bay leaf; then fill the pot up with clarified butter, covering the fish completely. Keep for a day or two before using. To keep for a longer period, up to 10 days, fill the butter up to the depth of 1/2 inch/ 1 cm over the top of the fish. Keep in the refrigerator.

Note: to clarify butter, melt the butter gently and allow it to stand until the sediment falls to the bottom. Carefully pour the clear butter over the fish, leaving the sediment behind.

Serves 6, as a starter

Dunguaire Castle, Galway Bay
Previous page: Croagh Mharainn, Co. Kerry

CRAB SOUP WITH SAFFRON

12 oz/340 g cooked
  crab meat
4–5 saffron strands
6 large scallions (spring
  onions), finely chopped
1 garlic clove
2 teaspoons fresh marjoram
1 oz/25 g butter
1¹/₂ pint/850 ml fish or light
  chicken stock
1 tablespoon long-grain rice
1 tablespoon grated lemon
  zest
¹/₄ pint/150 ml cream
1 tablespoon chopped fresh
  parsley, to garnish

Soak the saffron in a little water
for 30 minutes. Cook the finely
chopped scallions (spring onions),
garlic and marjoram in the butter,
until soft. Add the stock, rice,
lemon zest and saffron, with its
water, and simmer gently until the
rice is soft. Add the crab and the
cream and season well. Bring back
to the boil. Cook for 2–3 minutes
and then serve, garnished with the
parsley.

Serves 6

SCOTCH EGGS

*In spite of its name, this simple combination of eggs and pork has a long history
in Ireland and, though somewhat out of fashion, they are still popular for picnics and parties and summer
hors d'oeuvre. A simple mustard mayonnaise makes a good sauce. Scotch eggs also make a very
good lunch, served with buttery creamed potatoes.*

4 large eggs
7 oz/200 g pork, very finely
  minced, or good
  sausagemeat
3 scallions (spring onions)
1 oz/30 g butter
1 tablespoon cornflour
1 tablespoon Worcestershire
  sauce or soy sauce
1 tablespoon lemon juice
salt and pepper
oil, for deep-frying

FOR THE MUSTARD
MAYONNAISE
2 egg yolks, at room
  temperature
1 tablespoon mild French
  mustard
¹/₂ pint/275 ml olive oil
1 tablespoon horseradish
  cream (approx.)
salt

Boil the eggs for just 10 minutes in
plenty of water. Sauté the
chopped scallions (spring onions)
in the butter until soft. Allow to
cool. Mix the pork, scallions
(spring onions), cornflour, and
Worcestershire or soy sauce,
lemon juice and salt and pepper
together, to make a paste. Shell
the eggs and dry them carefully.
Divide the pork into 4 portions
and, with floured hands, shape
around each egg, encasing them
completely. Deep-fry the eggs in
sufficient oil to cover them, turning
frequently to prevent them from
splitting. About 6–8 minutes
should cook them. Drain on
kitchen paper.

For a starter or buffet, slice the
eggs lengthways and arrange on
crisp lettuce. For a picnic leave
them whole.

To make the mustard
mayonnaise, mix the egg yolks with
the mustard. Gradually pour in the
oil, drop by drop at first, and then
in a thin stream as it begins to
emulsify. Use a wooden spoon and
stir continuously, or use an electric
beater on medium speed. Season
well with a pinch of salt and add
creamed horseradish, to taste.
Should the mayonnaise separate,
put another egg yolk in a clean
bowl and add the mixture, drop
by drop, as before.

Serves 8, as a starter

Hill path, Co. Kerry

LOVAGE SOUP

Lovage, once to be found in every Irish garden, has celery-like leaves that make interesting soups and salads. Celery leaves can be prepared in the same way.

**2–3 large handfuls young
  lovage leaves
1 oz/30 g butter
1 onion, chopped
1 garlic clove, chopped
1 tablespoon plain flour
1 pint/560 ml hot chicken
  stock
1 pint/560 ml milk
3 teaspoons lemon juice
salt and freshly ground
  black pepper
fresh lovage leaves, to garnish
4 tablespoons croûtons**

Melt the butter in a large saucepan and cook the onion and garlic until soft. Add the chopped lovage and lemon juice. Cook until the leaves soften a little and then sprinkle in the flour. Continue stirring until the flour is cooked and the sauce is smooth. Gradually add half the hot stock, stirring well, until the flour has cooked. Purée in a food processor or blender. Return to the saucepan, add the rest of the stock and the milk and bring back to the boil. Season well with plenty of black pepper and salt to taste. Just before serving, garnish with a few fresh lovage leaves, and the croûtons.

Note: to make the croûtons, remove the crusts from 3 slices of white bread, cut into cubes and fry in a little oil, until brown. Drain on kitchen paper.

Serves 6

Ben Bulben, Co. Sligo

PEA POD SOUP

The pods of baby peas, so juicy and sweet, make very good soup, with an intense pea taste. Sugar-snap peas, now available in most supermarkets, give something of the same flavour.

8 oz/225 g sugar-snap peas
1 onion, finely chopped
1 oz/30 g butter
1 oz/30 g flour
1¼ pint/850 ml hot chicken
   or vegetable stock
fresh mint or summer savory,
   roughly chopped
½ teaspoon sugar
1 tablespoon chopped parsley
salt and freshly ground
   black pepper
3–4 tablespoons cream
chopped fresh mint, to
   garnish

Wash the peas and then just barely cover with water. Simmer until they are tender, about 15 minutes. Strain the peas and keep the water.

Cook the onion in the butter, until soft. Then mix in the flour and stir until cooked, 2–3 minutes.

Gradually add half the hot stock, stirring well until it thickens. Add the mint or savory. Put this mixture, with the peas, through the liquidiser or food processor and process until smooth. Return to the saucepan.

Add the remainder of the stock, the sugar, salt, pepper and parsley. Check the seasoning and bring to the boil for 2–3 minutes. A little of the pea water can be added, for a thinner soup. Serve in small bowls, with a little cream in each. Garnish with mint.

Serves 4

SMOKED SALMON PÂTÉ

12 oz/340 g smoked salmon
6 fl oz/175 ml crème fraîche
grated zest and juice of ¹/₂
    lemon
fresh dill sprigs
3 oz/75 g butter, melted
4 fl oz/110 ml double cream

TO DECORATE
small fresh dill sprigs
gherkins

Skin and chop the salmon,
removing any bones or hard
pieces. Put in a processor with the
crème fraîche, lemon zest and
juice, a few sprigs of dill and 2oz/
55g of the melted butter. Purée
until a smooth paste is formed, and
then gradually beat in the cream,
by hand.

Rub 6 little ramekins with oil and
pack the pâté into them. Brush the
tops with the remaining butter,
cover and chill.

To serve, decorate with dill and
gherkins. Serve with brown toast.
   Serves 6

White Bull Head, West Cork

CHICKEN, ORANGE AND ROCKET SALAD WITH WALNUT SAUCE

Large boneless, skinless
    chicken breasts, weighing
    about 1 lb/450 g in total
18–20 rocket leaves
2 large sweet oranges, 3 if
    small
¹/₂ pint/280 ml chicken stock
salt

FOR THE SAUCE
3¹/₂ oz/90 g walnut halves
1 tablespoon cider or sherry
    vinegar
3 tablespoons walnut or
    olive oil
2 teaspoons sugar
1 garlic clove
reserved stock

Place the chicken in a saucepan
and barely cover with the stock.
Add water, if necessary. Add a
pinch of salt and poach gently until
cooked but still juicy, about 10–15
minutes. Shred the chicken by
pulling it apart with 2 forks,
lengthways, with the grain of the
meat. Strain the stock and reserve
for the sauce.

Wash and dry the rocket leaves
and leave in the refrigerator
to crisp.

To make the sauce, toast the
walnuts in a dry pan until crisp and
very slightly brown. Put them in a
blender, with the other sauce
ingredients and half the reserved
stock. Grind to a smooth paste.
Adjust to taste, adding more
vinegar or sugar as required. Dilute
to a thin purée with some of the
remaining stock. Reserve 2
tablespoons of sauce to finish.
Peel the oranges with a sharp knife
and then slice down between the
sections, separating the flesh from
the dividing membrane. Allow 2 or
3 slices per person. All of this can
be prepared ahead of time, or the
day before.

To serve, pour a small pool of
sauce on each plate and arrange
some of the chicken, orange and
rocket on each. Thin the remaining
2 tablespoons of sauce with more
stock or oil and drizzle over the
top.
   Serves 6, as a starter

SUMMER
main courses

CHICKEN AND HAM PASTIES

The combination of chicken and ham is perennially popular in Ireland. These old-fashioned pasties make an excellent lunch or simple dinner and are indispensable picnic fare. Serve with new potatoes and a salad.

8 oz/225 g cooked chicken, finely chopped

8 oz/225 g cooked ham, finely chopped

2 small leeks, finely chopped

3¹/₂ oz/90 g mushrooms, sliced

2 oz/55 g butter

1 tablespoon plain flour

¹/₂ pint/280 ml hot milk

¹/₂ teaspoon coriander seeds

1 teaspoon poppy seeds

salt and freshly ground black pepper

FOR THE PASTRY
14 oz/400 g plain flour

8 oz/225 g butter

1 small egg, beaten, to glaze

salt, pinch

Preheat the oven to 190°C/375°F/Gas Mark 5. Make the pastry in the usual way by rubbing the butter into the flour and salt and moistening with 2-4 tablespoons of cold water. Roll out into four 6 inch/15 cm circles. Chill.

Sauté the leeks with the mushrooms in 1 oz/30 g of the butter. Set aside.

Melt the remaining butter in a saucepan, stir in the flour, cook for 2 minutes and then gradually add the hot milk, stirring continuously until the sauce thickens smoothly. Season well. Add the coriander seeds and the leek mixture and its juices. Cool.

Fold the finely chopped meats into the sauce, when it is cool, and divide between the pastry circles. Dampen the edges and draw the 2 sides together, pinching well to seal. Place, seam-side down, on a greased baking sheet. Brush with beaten egg and sprinkle with poppy seeds. Bake until the pastry is golden, about 20–25 minutes. Serve hot or cold.

Serves 4

MACKEREL WITH GOOSEBERRY SAUCE

This is another combination that has its origins in the past, when fruit sauces with fish or meat were considered good for the digestion. Apple sauce with pork is another example. The elderflowers give a delicate muscatel flavour and were often added to apple and gooseberry tarts. Pick the elderflowers well away from dusty roadsides. The sauce can be hot or cold, as you prefer, and is equally good with kippers or pork.

6 mackerel, scaled and cleaned

1 lb/450 g gooseberries

1–2 heads of elderflowers

2–3 tablespoons water

sugar to taste

2 tablespoons plain flour

1 egg, beaten

3 tablespoons fine oatmeal

butter and oil, for frying

salt and freshly ground black pepper

Cook the gooseberries and elderflowers with 2–3 tablespoons of water, until soft. Remove the elderflowers, sweeten to taste and push through a sieve. Set aside.

Clean the mackerel, wash and dry, removing heads if preferred. Season the insides and flour well. Dip the mackerel in the beaten egg and roll in the oatmeal. Melt a tablespoon each of butter and oil in a large frying-pan and fry the mackerel over a low heat, until the flesh is opaque. Drain on kitchen paper and serve with the gooseberry sauce and creamy mashed potatoes, to which you have added finely chopped spring onions and lots of black pepper.

Serves 6

Slea Head, Co. Kerry

BAKED SALMON WITH A HERB CRUST

Though excellent farmed salmon is available all year round, the creamy, curdy texture of wild salmon in May is perfection.

3–5 lb/1.35 kg–2.25 kg
  salmon, in 2 fillets, skinned
3 tablespoons finely chopped
  fresh parsley
3 tablespoons finely chopped
  scallions (spring onions)
1 inch/2.5 cm cube of fresh
  root ginger
6 tinned anchovy fillets,
  drained
4 oz/110 g butter
grated zest of 1 lemon
3 oz/75 g breadcrumbs, made
  from day-old bread

FOR THE SAUCE
3 egg yolks
$^1/_2$ pint/280 ml cream
5–6 sorrel leaves, ribs
  removed, leaves chopped
grated zest of 1 lemon
salt and freshly ground
  black pepper
1 tablespoon fresh chopped
  coriander or parsley

Preheat the oven to 170°C/325°F/Gas Mark 3. Mash the ginger to a paste with the anchovies, 3 oz/75 g of butter, scallions (spring onions), parsley and the grated zest of half the lemon. Butter a sheet of baking parchment which will fit the salmon and line a baking tray. Lay one fillet of salmon on the paper and spread with half the herb butter. Lay the other fillet on top, reversing the wide end over the narrow end of the bottom fillet. Spread the remaining herb butter on top.

Cover the salmon with the breadcrumbs, patting them down lightly; season well and dot with the remaining 1 oz/30 g of butter. Bake for 12 minutes per 1 lb/450 g, for smaller fish, but a 6–7 lb fish will not require more than an hour.

When cooked, use the baking paper to lift the fish on to a heated serving dish. Retain the juices for the sauce.

To make the sauce, season the egg yolks and beat together. Bring the cream to a boil, with the sorrel leaves and lemon zest and cook to reduce for a few moments. Pour on to the yolks, stirring well and then return to the saucepan and, over a low heat, cook, stirring continuously and without allowing it to boil, until the sauce thickens slightly. Pour the strained fish juices into the sauce, add the coriander or parsley and serve.

Serves 6 as a main course, or 8–10 as part of a buffet

SCALLOPS WITH TARRAGON SAUCE

Tender, juicy scallops need very little cooking. Be sure to save the red corals when cleaning them.

12 scallops, cleaned
6 fl oz/175 ml white wine
3 fl oz/100 ml water
grated zest and juice of $^1/_2$
lemon
4–5 fresh tarragon leaves or a
pinch of dried tarragon
3 fl oz/100 ml cream
$^1/_2$ **oz/15 g butter**
3 egg yolks, beaten
1 tablespoon chopped fresh
parsley

Put the wine, water, lemon juice and zest and tarragon leaves together in a saucepan and boil for 2–3 minutes. Add the scallops and corals and gently poach for about 5 minutes, until they are no longer translucent and are firm to the touch. Remove to a warm place.

Strain the cooking liquid into a small saucepan and boil rapidly, to reduce slightly. Add the cream and butter and boil for 2–3 minutes. Then pour on to the egg yolks, whisking well all the time. Return the mixture to the saucepan over a very low heat and continue to stir until the sauce thickens slightly. Do not allow to boil. Season well, add the parsley and more tarragon, if desired.

Arrange the scallops on warm plates and pour the sauce over them. Creamy mashed potatoes are the classic companion for scallops.

Serves 3–4 as a main course, depending on the size of the scallops, or 6 as a starter

Oughterard house front, Co. Galway

HAM IN PASTRY

*Hams, and the art of cooking them, are well understood in Ireland and they are always
popular for grand occasions. If the ham is to be eaten hot, seasonal vegetables and a well made
parsley sauce are the traditional partners. Rowanberry jelly, heated with a glass of port and
a little orange juice, also makes an excellent sauce.*

**6–8 lb/2.8–3.6 kg fillet of ham,
bone removed**

**2 lb/900 g puff or shortcrust
pastry**

1 large onion, halved

2–3 tablespoons brown sugar

1 tablespoon mustard powder

**2 tablespoons Dijon-type mild
mustard**

1 egg, beaten, to glaze

2 bay leaves

juniper berries

Soak the ham overnight in cold
water if it seems to be salty;
otherwise 1–2 hours will do.

When ready to cook, put the
ham in a large saucepan, with a few
juniper berries, the bay leaves and
the onion halves. Add the sugar and
mustard powder, cover with cold
water and, timing from when the
water boils, simmer for 20 minutes
per 1 lb/450 g. Test for tenderness
with a skewer before the last 20
minutes, as they may not be
necessary. The ham will cook a little
more in the oven. When cooked,
allow to cool for about 30 minutes
in the water, then remove and peel
off the skin and some of the fat if
there is too much. Allow the ham
to cool further. Preheat the oven
to 190°C/375°F/Gas Mark 5.
Roll out the pastry into a large
square that will cover the ham,
keeping it a little thicker than usual
– about ¼ inch/0.5 cm. Rub Dijon
mustard over the ham and then
cover it completely with the pastry,
trimming the surplus and
dampening and sealing the joins.
Place on a baking tray, keeping the
seams underneath as far as
possible.

Brush over with the beaten egg.
Use the trimmings to make leaves
etc. and brush over with the egg
again. Make a vent at the highest
point.

Bake for about 20 minutes.
Cover the pastry loosely with foil,
lower the heat to
170°C/325°F/Gas Mark 3 for
another 45 minutes or so, to
ensure the ham is completely
heated through.

*Serves 10 as a main course, 25 as
part of a buffet*

Upper Caragh River, Co. Kerry

JELLIED TONGUE

Liked and disliked with equal intensity, a pressed beef tongue is an essential ingredient of any Irish cold meat platter and, though it takes a long time to cook, the preparation is extremely simple. A little port added to the stock gives a richer jelly. Small, ready-trimmed tongues are widely available and do not usually require soaking; larger tongues may need soaking overnight.

**1 tongue, weighing about
  2 lb/900 g
1 each onion, carrot and
  celery stick
2 teaspoons black peppercorns
1 orange
a glass of port
4 teaspoons/11 g or 0.4 oz
  sachet/3 leaves gelatine**

Place the tongue in a large saucepan and cover with cold water. Add the vegetables, peppercorns and a large strip of orange zest. Bring to the boil very slowly and simmer gently, until a skewer will slide in easily. This can take from 2–4 hours, depending on its size. Remove the tongue from the water when cool enough to handle and peel off the skin and any gristle. Return the tongue to the stock, to keep warm.

Strain off ½ pint/280 ml of the cooking liquid and use a little to dissolve the gelatine, according to the packet directions. Put the remainder in a small saucepan, with the port and the juice of 1/2 orange. Boil hard to reduce for 1–2 minutes; then add the dissolved gelatine. Put the warm tongue in a bowl or mould that will just hold it. Pour over enough of the port jelly to cover it when it is pressed down well with a plate or saucer. Put a weight on top of the plate (tin cans or a stone) and leave overnight. Put the remaining port jelly to set, for the garnish.

To serve, remove any fat from the top, and then turn out the tongue and carve in thin slices. Decorate with the chopped jelly. Spicy Cumberland sauce or horseradish cream can be served with it and Pickled Hard-Boiled Eggs (see page 61), too.

Serves 6 as a main course, 8–10 as part of a buffet

R A G O U T   O F
S C A L L O P S
A N D   B A C O N

8 scallops, cleaned
4 streaky bacon rashers
1 oz/30 g butter
1 onion, chopped
2–3 scallions (spring onions),
    chopped
8 oz/225 g mixed shiitake and
    oyster mushrooms
2 teaspoons plain flour
$^1/_4$ pint/150 ml white wine
$^1/_4$ pint/150 ml cream
1 tablespoon chopped fresh
    parsley
1 teaspoon chopped fresh dill
    or chervil
1 tablespoon lemon juice
salt and pepper

Remove the red corals, and then
slice the scallops into 3 pieces,
horizontally. Sauté them gently
with the corals for 1–2 minutes in
half the butter. Fry the bacon until
crisp; then chop finely. Cook the
onion and mushrooms in the
bacon fat, adding the remaining
butter, for 2–3 minutes; then
sprinkle in the flour, stirring well
until the flour is cooked. Stir in the
wine and bubble until the sauce
thickens, then add the cream,
bacon, parsley, dill and a little
lemon juice. Check the seasoning
and bring back to the boil. Add the
scallops and allow to heat through,
about 2–3 minutes.
    Serves 4

PICKLED HARD-BOILED EGGS

In the not-too-distant past, when Irish pubs were quiet retreats for serious drinking men and 'pub grub' hadn't been thought of, large jars of pickled eggs stood on old bar counters, luminescent in the near-silent gloom, the only concession to food.

Hard-boil the eggs by placing them in a large saucepan of cold water. Bring the water to the boil and then remove it from the heat and leave to stand, covered, for 15 minutes. Remove the eggs to cold running water and peel carefully.

When completely cold, put them in large jam jars, which have plastic-lined lids, and cover them completely with white-wine vinegar. Add a few peppercorns to each jar. White malt vinegar can also be used. Leave for several days before using.

Kilkenny, a town rich in pubs

PEAS AND LETTUCE

This combination of two summer vegetables is more than 200 years old and, though its origins are French, it is to be found in almost every Irish family recipe collection of the past. Nowadays, it need not wait for summer, frozen petits pois make a reasonable substitute for the tender young summer peas – and can be used straight away, without blanching. This vegetable dish is equally delicious eaten with fish or meat.

1 lb/450 g petits pois, thawed, or tender young fresh peas, blanched
a head of butterhead-type lettuce (with a heart)
2 oz/55 g butter
3–4 scallions (spring onions), finely chopped
chopped fresh chervil or summer savory
ground mace or grated nutmeg
salt and freshly ground black pepper

Wash and dry the lettuce. Stack the leaves on top of each other, roll up gently and cut at 1 inch/ 2.5 cm intervals, to give strips.

Melt the butter in a saucepan and gently cook the scallions (spring onions). Add the peas, lettuce, herbs and seasonings and cook very gently for about 10 minutes.

Serves 6

The Blasket Islands from Slea Head, Co. Kerry

ROAST BEEF SALAD

A fillet of Irish beef needs little adornment and is at its best simply prepared. For this summery salad, both beef and sauce can be prepared well in advance.

FOR THE SALAD
1¹/₂ lb/675 g beef fillet,
    in one piece
4 tablespoons olive oil
2 tablespoons red wine vinegar
2 garlic cloves, crushed
2 teaspoons ground allspice
1 tablespoon Dijon mustard
2 bunches scallions (spring
    onions)
mixed lettuce, herb leaves,
    cherry tomatoes, marigold
    petals, chive or rocket flowers

FOR THE SAUCE
4 tablespoons white wine
    vinegar
1 teaspoon peppercorns
4 tablespoons water
4 egg yolks
6 oz/170 g unsalted butter,
    softened
2 teaspoons each chopped
    fresh tarragon and parsley,
    mixed

Trim the meat of any fat and tie it around at intervals, to keep its shape while cooking. Marinate the meat at room temperature in the oil, vinegar and crushed garlic for 2–3 hours.

Preheat the oven to 220°C/425°F/Gas Mark 7. Remove the beef from the marinade and wipe dry with kitchen paper. Mix the allspice and mustard together and spread over the meat. Roast the meat for 20 minutes. This will give pink beef. Cook for 5–7 minutes longer if preferred. Five minutes before the end of the cooking time, brush the scallions (spring onions) with more olive oil

and scatter over the meat. Remove the meat and cool quickly.

To make the sauce, boil the vinegar, peppercorns and 1 teaspoon of the herbs, with the water, until reduced to 2 tablespoons. Strain into a small bowl over hot water, or use a double-boiler, and beat in the egg yolks. Stir well until the yolks are warm; then gradually stir in the softened butter, in walnut-sized lumps, stirring until the sauce thickens slightly and will coat the back of a spoon. Stir continually, lifting the saucepan on and off the heat to prevent it from overheating and scrambling the eggs. When the sauce has thickened, pour it into a blender and whizz for a few moments, until it becomes slightly foamy. Add the remaining herbs, cover and set aside. If there is no blender, whisk hard with a wire whisk. Pour into a sauce boat or dish.

Arrange the lettuce and leaves attractively on a large serving dish. Untie the beef and slice very thinly. Arrange in an overlapping circle and put the wilted scallions (spring onions) in the centre. (The beef will lose its colour if sliced too soon.) Garnish with the tomatoes and whatever herb flowers are to hand, marigold petals, chive or rocket flowers. Spoon a little vinaigrette over the leaves just before serving.

SUMMER
desserts

STRAWBERRIES IN CLARET JELLY

Eating strawberries with red wine is a very old custom, the acidity of both being tempered by the liberal use of sugar and spice. Choose a wine you like to drink.
'How I like Claret! When I can get Claret, I must drink it....
If you could make some wine like Claret to drink on summer evenings in an arbour ...'
John Keats, letter to his brother, 1819

12 oz/340 g strawberries
1 pint/575 ml claret or other
  red wine
8 teaspoons/2 x 11 g or
  0.4 oz sachets/6 leaves
  gelatine
7 oz/200 g redcurrant jelly
4 oz/110 g caster sugar,
  or to taste
1 cinnamon stick
2–3 tablespoons water
2 tablespoons brandy
2 tablespoons lemon juice
strawberries and fruits,
  to decorate

Wipe the strawberries with kitchen paper, and hull them. Put 3–4 tablespoons of the wine in a small bowl and sprinkle the gelatine over it. When the gelatine has softened, stand the bowl in hot water and stir until the gelatine has completely dissolved. Keep warm.

Heat the redcurrant jelly, the sugar and cinnamon stick in a saucepan with the water, until both sugar and jelly have dissolved. Remove the cinnamon and strain into a large bowl. Add the gelatine and mix thoroughly. When cool add the claret, brandy and lemon juice. Pour half the mixture and half the strawberries into a dampened 2 pint/1.2 litre jelly mould and chill when cool.

Warm the remaining jelly mixture, add the rest of the strawberries and fill up the mould. (If this operation is done all at once, the strawberries will float to the top.) Chill when cool. Turn out when completely set and decorate with fruits, flowers and leaves.

Have a bowl of whipped cream on hand, for those who like it. One or 2 geranium leaves, infused in the cream for an hour or so, give a subtle flavour.

Serves 6

Garinish Island, Co. Cork

STRAWBERRY CHOCOLATE ROLL

Swiss rolls and chocolate rolls are a favourite component of the Irish tea table. This strawberry-filled chocolate roll is rich enough for an elegant summer dinner party.

FOR THE CAKE
3 oz/75 g plain flour
1 oz/30 g cocoa powder
¹/₂ teaspoon baking powder
2 large eggs
4 oz/110 g caster sugar
2 tablespoons hot water
icing sugar, sifted, to decorate

FOR THE FILLING
1 lb/450 g strawberries,
  cleaned and hulled
8 fl oz/225 ml double cream
2 oz/55 g caster sugar
brandy or vanilla essence

Preheat the oven to 220°C/425°F/Gas Mark 7. Butter a 12 x 9 inch/30 x 23 cm swiss-roll tin and line with baking parchment. Cut another piece of parchment the same size and have ready a tea-towel, wrung out in hot water.

Sift the flour, cocoa and baking powder. Beat the eggs and sugar together until thick, white and creamy. With a large metal spoon, fold in the flour, cutting with the edge of the spoon, and turning, rather than mixing. Finally, fold in the hot water. Pour into the tin, smooth with a palette knife and bake for 7–10 minutes, until the mixture has slightly shrunk away from the sides. If the sponge is overcooked, it becomes dry.

Put the piece of baking parchment on the hot tea-towel and sprinkle it with sugar. Turn the cake out on top. Quickly trim the edges, peel the baking paper away carefully and roll up, with the paper inside. Leave to cool.

Stiffly whip the cream with a little sugar and brandy or vanilla essence. Roughly chop three-quarters of the strawberries and fold them into the cream. Carefully unroll the chocolate roll, remove the paper and fill with the strawberry mixture. Roll up the cake and dredge with a little icing sugar. Decorate with the remaining strawberries.

Serves 6

Sligo thatch

ROSE-PETAL ICE CREAM

Scented roses are one of the great pleasures of summer. To make the most of them when they are at their peak, try this romantic ice cream.

1 pint/575 ml red or pink scented rose petals
4 oz/110 g caster sugar
¹/₄ pint/150 ml rosé wine
5 egg yolks
1 vanilla pod or 1 teaspoon vanilla essence
¹/₂ pint/280 ml milk
¹/₂ pint/280 ml double cream
1 teaspoon rose-water (obtainable in oriental grocers)
crystallised rose petals, to decorate (see below)

To prepare the rose petals, wipe them clean with damp kitchen paper and cut away the hard white stem or heel. Put them in a blender or food processor, with 2 oz/55 g of the sugar and the wine, and purée.

Beat the eggs and remaining sugar thoroughly. Split the vanilla pod, if using, and add to the milk and cream. Bring to the boil and simmer gently for a few moments, to infuse. Remove the pod (add vanilla essence now, if using). Pour the hot mixture on to the eggs and sugar and return to the saucepan, stirring continuously. Heat to just below boiling point. Do not let it boil. The point is reached when, removing the spoon from the mixture and running the finger along it, the mixture remains separated. Leave to cool.

Mix in the rose purée and rose-water. Taste for sweetness. Freeze in the usual way, by stirring and beating the mixture 2 or 3 times during the freezing process. To serve, decorate with crystallised rose petals.

Note: to make crystallised rose petals, prepare the rose petals as for the ice cream. Beat one large egg white, until just fluid. Dip each petal into the egg white and then dredge in caster sugar covering completely. Spread the petals on a foil-lined baking tray and dry in a very low oven, with the door ajar, for an hour or so, until they are crisp. Store in an airtight tin, between sheets of greaseproof paper. Use for cake decoration also.

Serves 4

A Donegal window

CHERRY MOUSSE

1 lb/450 g cherries
1 tablespoon each grated
   lemon zest and lemon juice
4 teaspoons/11 g or 0.4 oz
   sachet/3 leaves gelatine
4 eggs
2 oz/55 g caster sugar
¹/₄ pint/150 ml whipping
   cream
summer fruits or fresh mint
   leaves, to decorate

Poach the cherries in as little water as possible until soft enough to extract the stones. Purée the cherries, with 1–2 tablespoons of their juice and the lemon zest and juice. Use the remainder to dissolve the gelatine, according to the directions on the packet.

Separate the eggs and put the yolks and sugar in a bowl over hot water. Whisk, over a low heat, until thick and creamy. Remove from the heat and whisk from time to time, until cool. Cool the gelatine and stir thoroughly into the egg mixture; then beat in the cherry purée. Lightly whip the cream and fold it in. Whisk the egg whites to the soft-peak stage and, when the gelatine mixture is on the point of setting, fold the whites in carefully, amalgamating them thoroughly.

Divide the mousse between 6 ring moulds or ramekins and allow to set. Decorate with berries or mint leaves.

Serves 6

Syllabub

In the seventeenth century, this was a popular confection of wine, cider or fruit juice to which milk was added by force, often by milking the cow directly into the other ingredients to make froth, or bubbles. Nowadays, it takes only minutes to prepare. In earlier times syllabub was the traditional covering for trifle, before the use of whipped cream became universal, and macaroons often formed the base.

$^1/_2$ **pint/280 ml whipping cream**
3 tablespoons sweet white wine or sherry
juice of $^1/_2$ orange
grated zest of $^1/_2$ lemon
2 oz/55 g caster sugar

TO DECORATE
summer fruits
Macaroons (see page 103)

Whip all the ingredients together until thick and creamy. Carefully spoon into four glasses. Make the syllabub a few hours in advance, to allow the flavours to develop. Garnish with berries and serve with macaroons.
Serves 4

LOGANBERRY AND PLUM JAM

It seems more like fun to make small quantities of different jams with whatever is to hand and this intensely flavoured combination is well worth the half hour it takes. If there are no gooseberries, use more lemon juice.

1 lb/450 g plums
1 lb/450 g loganberries
4 oz/110 g gooseberries
juice of ¹/₂ lemon
2 lb/900 g caster sugar
15 fl oz/425 ml water

Simmer the plums and gooseberries in the water, until the plums are soft enough to remove the stones. Cut the plums in pieces, if they are large, and return them to the water.

Add the loganberries, bring back to the boil and cook for 5 minutes. Remove from the heat, pour in the sugar and lemon juice and stir until completely dissolved. Boil hard for 7–10 minutes, until a few drops cooled on a chilled saucer will wrinkle when pushed with the finger. Pour into hot, sterilised pots and cover.

Makes 5 x 8 oz/225 g jars

Summer cows

Summer

RASPBERRY JAM

The raspberry season is so short but jams and preserves help to prolong the taste of summer.

3 lb/1.4 kg raspberries
3 lb/1.4 kg caster sugar
8 oz/225 g redcurrants or
  2 tablespoons lemon juice

Put the caster sugar into an ovenproof dish and warm gently in the oven.

Put the fruit in a stainless steel saucepan over a very low heat, until the juice begins to flow; then bring very slowly to the boil and simmer for 10 minutes. Pour in the warmed sugar and lemon juice, if using, and stir until the sugar has completely dissolved. Then boil hard until it sets when tested. Start testing after 8 minutes. Put some saucers to chill in the freezer and then test by putting a few drops of the mixture on a saucer and allowing to cool. If the surface of the drop wrinkles when pushed with a finger, the jam is ready. Pot in hot, dry, sterilised jars and seal immediately.

Makes 5 x 12 oz/335 g jars

ROSE-PETAL VINEGAR

Use this delicate vinegar to flavour summer salads, or try a few drops on summer fruits, such as strawberries and raspberries; it seems to bring out the flavours.

The choice of the base vinegar is important. Use a good-quality white-wine vinegar, or organic cider vinegar. Rice vinegar, which can be bought from oriental shops, is particularly delicate in flavour. Measure equal quantities of vinegar and scented rose petals, about 2 large cupfuls of each. Put them together in a glass or porcelain container and cover tightly. They should be left to steep on a sunny window for at least 3 weeks. If you like a stronger flavour, strain off the petals and add fresh ones; then steep a little longer. Strain into bottles and cork tightly. Elderflower vinegar can be made the same way.

Serves 6

Haycocks, Co. Kerry
Overleaf: Killarney, Co. Kerry

AUTUMN

AUGUST is the month when the lazy beds gave up their new potatoes; this was once a significant date, but is now unnoticed, when potatoes of all sizes and ages, from all over Europe and, apparently, independent of season, are in the shops.

Oysters, too, are taken from their beds (the superb native oyster even merits its own festival in Galway at this time of year) and will be plentiful and good during the autumn and winter, when they'll be consumed in quantity and washed down with Guinness. In the days before tea became the other national beverage, when cider and beer were consumed by young and old, apple and pear orchards were abundant in the countryside. Some of these areas still retain their fame: Armagh has given its name to many apple dishes, as has Clonmel, where excellent cider is still made today.

Mushrooms make their appearance in late summer and early autumn and their mysterious nature has been a source of fascination from earliest times. The rapidity of growth, the fact they appear to grow at night and are there, waiting, in the early morning, has given rise to a wide folklore and numerous old wives' tales, such as using a silver spoon when cooking mushrooms — it was supposed to turn black if the mushrooms were poisonous. Hallowe'en is the climax of autumn and, perhaps, the favourite festival of children. Old traditions live on and apples, studded with coins, and floating in bowls of water, are still bobbed for. Dressing up, wearing masks and carving pumpkins (it used to be turnips) are as popular as ever. Colcannon is made, and slices of brack are scrutinised in hopes of finding a ring and a sweetheart; fortunes are told, and there are bonfires too. Best of all, perhaps, for the young, there is a break from school.

AUTUMN
starters

MUSHROOMS IN PASTRY

There is a charm in mushrooms that is never quite dispelled by familiarity. Use as many kinds as you can find; their different flavours blend together interestingly.

1 lb/450 g mixed mushrooms
12 oz/340 g frozen or
  homemade puff pastry
8 oz/225 g spinach
2–3 oz/55–75 g butter
1 garlic clove, finely chopped
2 tablespoons mushroom
  ketchup
$^1/_2$ teaspoon Cayenne pepper
1 egg, beaten
$^1/_4$ pint/150 ml cream
salt and freshly ground
  black pepper

Preheat the oven to 190°C/375°F/Gas Mark 5. Wash and coarsely chop the spinach. Melt a knob of butter in a large frying pan and gently cook the garlic for a few moments, and then add the spinach and toss until it is softly wilted. Remove and squeeze any juices back into the pan.

Wipe and trim the mushrooms and chop them coarsely. Add another tablespoon of butter and one of ketchup to the pan and cook the mushrooms until they are reduced but still juicy. Season well with salt, pepper and cayenne. (If oyster mushrooms are used don't put them in until the last moment.) Remove the mushrooms to cool but leave the juices in the pan.

Roll out the pastry into 2 large rectangles about 9 x 6 inch/23 x 15 cm. Place one on a greased baking sheet and cover it with the spinach, then pile on the mushrooms, leaving a $^1/_2$ inch/ 1 cm space around the edges. Dot with butter and then cover with the other rectangle of pastry. Press the dampened edges together and make a vent in the top. Brush with the beaten egg. Bake until golden, about 40 minutes.

Add the cream, remaining butter and a tablespoon of mushroom ketchup to the juices in the pan and bubble for a few moments, to make a little sauce.

*Serves 4 as a main course,
or 8 as a starter*

*The Paps, Co. Kerry
Previous page: near Bantry, Co. Cork*

SMOKED SALMON TARTLETS

*These delicate little tartlets, filled with smoked salmon mousse, can be garnished with whatever
suits taste and season: anchovies and capers, quail's eggs or salmon roes.*

FOR THE PASTRY
10 oz/275 g plain flour
**¹/₂ teaspoon grated lemon
   zest**
5 oz/140 g butter
1 egg yolk
1 tablespoon very cold water
salt

FOR THE FILLING
8 oz/225 g smoked salmon
**8 fl oz/225 ml crème fraîche
   or double cream**
**2 teaspoons finely chopped
   fresh dill or tarragon**
¹/₂ teaspoon paprika
2 teaspoons lemon juice
Tabasco or chilli sauce
**fresh chervil or tarragon
   leaves, to garnish**

TO SERVE
mixed salad leaves
oil and balsamic vinegar

To make the pastry, sift the flour
with a pinch of salt, stir in the
lemon rind and rub in the butter.
Moisten with the egg yolk and a
tablespoon of cold water. Chill for
half an hour.

Preheat the oven to
190°C/375°F/Gas Mark 5. Roll out
the pastry to fit six 3 inch/8 cm
buttered tartlet tins. Prick the
bottoms. Line with baking
parchment and then fit the tins
into each other, putting an empty
tin (or foil and dried beans) into
the top tin. Bake for 15 minutes.
Then remove from the oven,
separate and put back for a further
5 minutes or so, until crisp but not
too brown. These can be made in
advance and kept in a tin. Don't fill
them, however, until shortly before
serving, so they remain crisp.

Put the salmon and crème
fraîche or cream in the blender or
food processor, with the herbs,
paprika, lemon juice and a dash of
Tabasco or chilli sauce. Process
until a stiff purée is formed. Add a
little more cream, if it's too stiff.
Chill until required.

Divide the filling between the
pastry shells and arrange the
garnish on top. Mix the oil and
vinegar, to make a vinaigrette
dressing. Arrange some salad
leaves, dressed with a little
vinaigrette, on each plate and place
a tart beside the leaves, sprinkling a
few more drops of vinaigrette
around the plate.

Serves 6

An Súgán, well known for its seafood, in Clonakilty, Co. Cork

DEVILLED PRAWNS

'Devils', highly spiced morsels of fish or fowl, were hugely popular in Ireland in the past, for supper or after dinner, when they were considered as a stimulant to the punch bowl, or before dinner, as a spur to a jaded appetite. Numerous recipes for the definitive 'devil' were exchanged, many of tear-compelling pungency.

12 large raw prawns
2 limes or 1 lemon
1 teaspoon sea salt
1 teaspoon cayenne pepper
1 teaspoon paprika
1 teaspoon ground cumin
2 tablespoons melted butter
mustard powder (optional)

Peel the body shells from the prawns but leave the tails intact. To make the 'devil', mix the salt and spices together and form into a paste with the melted butter, the grated zest of one lime or ¹/₂ a lemon and a little juice. To make it hotter add more cayenne or a little mustard powder. Marinate the prawns in this mixture for a couple of hours.

Cook under a medium grill, until the prawns are cooked and the tail shells are pink. Garnish with lime or lemon slices. If cooked prawns are used, grill them just sufficiently to heat them through thoroughly.

Serves 4, as a starter

BLACK PUDDING PATTIES

*Puddings, black and white, are usually eaten at breakfast. These patties
make an unusual starter.*

12 oz/340 g Clonakilty black
  pudding
8 oz/225 g freshly cooked
  potato
4 scallions, finely chopped
1 beaten egg
1 large cooking apple, peeled
  and grated or chopped
2 large eating apples
2 oz/50 g butter
2 tablespoons brown flour
3 tablespoons oil for frying
small glass of white wine,
  vermouth or stock
salt and freshly ground
  black pepper
rocket or watercress to garnish

Peel the casing from the black
pudding and finely crumble it into a
mixing bowl. Mash in the potato,
the finely chopped scallions, the
grated apple, 1 oz of the butter

and the beaten egg. Mix well
together and form into 12 patties,
adding a tablespoon or so of milk if
the mixture is too dry. Dust with
the brown flour and fry gently in
the oil until hot and crisp. Keep
warm.

Wash the eating apples and cut
across into ½ inch/1 cm slices.
Stamp out the cores. In another
pan fry the apple slices in the
remaining butter until beginning to
brown but not breaking up.

Arrange these on the plates, two
per person and place the patties
on top. Pour the wine into the pan
and bubble well to deglaze the
pan. Pour the juices around the
patties. Garnish with the rocket,
watercress or other leaves.

Serves 6 as a starter

Conor Pass on the Dingle Peninsula

CHESTNUT AND LENTIL SOUP

This lovely soup is redolent of the season, with its warm colour and earthy flavours. A glass of not too dry sherry, an amontillado, perhaps, is excellent with this, a fashion which is due for revival.

8 oz/225 g prepared chestnuts (see page 84)

6 oz/170 g green or brown lentils

2 streaky bacon rashers, finely chopped

2 large onions, finely chopped

2 garlic cloves, finely chopped

2 oz/50 g butter

3 celery sticks, with leaves, chopped

1 carrot, grated

1 teaspoon ground cumin

2 pints/1.2 litres chicken or vegetable stock

$^1/_4$ pint/150 ml cream, to serve

salt and freshly ground black pepper

Put the bacon, onions and garlic in a large saucepan with the butter and sauté until the bacon is cooked and the onions are soft. Add the chopped celery (reserve the leaves) and carrot and cook for 3–4 minutes. Stir in the chestnuts which have been puréed in a blender with 4 tablespoons water.

Add the lentils, cumin and the stock to the saucepan and simmer gently, until the lentils are soft. Reserve 1–2 cupfuls of the soup, to give a little texture, and purée the remainder. Return to the reserved soup and season well. Reheat and serve with a spoonful of cream in each bowl, and the chopped celery leaves (or parsley) sprinkled over the top.

Serves 6

AUTUMN
main courses

BRAISED PHEASANTS WITH IRISH WHISKEY SAUCE

Pheasants are in season from October to January and are usually plentiful during this period.
Braising the birds keeps them moist and tender.

2 pheasants
3 oz/75 g butter
6 celery sticks, roughly
   chopped
4 carrots, roughly chopped
4 onions, roughly chopped
fresh parsley and thyme
   sprigs
1/2 pint/280 ml chicken
   stock
4 tablespoons redcurrant jelly
a large glass of Irish whiskey
1/2 pint/280 ml cream
salt and freshly ground
   black pepper

FOR THE STUFFING
4 oz/110 g hazelnuts
2 oz/55 g butter
1 tablespoon each finely
   chopped carrot, celery
   and onion
2 streaky bacon strips,
   chopped
1 orange
6 tablespoons cooked wild

and basmati rice mixture
1 tablespoon Irish whiskey
chestnuts and game chips,
   to garnish (optional, see
   below)

To make the stuffing, lightly brown the hazelnuts in a heavy pan, rub off any loose skins and chop finely. In the same pan, melt a knob of butter and sauté the chopped vegetables and bacon. Grate the zest of the orange and mix together with the other ingredients, rice and remaining butter. Moisten with a tablespoon each of whiskey and orange juice. Season well. When the mixture is cold, stuff the birds loosely and seal with a cocktail stick.

In a heavy casserole that will just fit the two birds, melt 2 oz/55 g of butter and brown the birds all over. Remove. Put in the roughly chopped vegetables and a few sprigs of parsley and thyme. Lay

the birds on top, on their sides, and pour on the stock. Season the birds well. Cover the casserole, sealing it well with foil, if necessary. Cook gently for 20 minutes. Then turn the pheasants and cook for a further 15–20 minutes. Test by inserting a skewer between the leg and the breast. The liquid should be faintly pink; pheasants do not benefit from overcooking. Remove the birds and keep them warm.

Strain off the liquid from the vegetables and remove as much fat as possible. Blend the liquid with the redcurrant jelly and pour into a small saucepan. Add the whiskey, heat for a few moments, and then ignite to burn off the alcohol and concentrate the flavour. Now add the cream, taste for seasoning, and boil hard to reduce. Finally, whisk in a little butter.

Arrange the birds on a large

serving dish, tuck the feathers under the tails (see photograph), if you have them, and glaze with a little of the sauce.

Pheasants are traditionally garnished with chestnuts and game chips, or served on a bed of spinach, finished in butter and garlic.

Game chips are made by slicing peeled potatoes very thinly into cold water. Remove from the water, dry and fry in hot oil. Drain and sprinkle with salt.

Note: to prepare chestnuts, make a cross in the skins with a sharp knife and boil for 20 minutes; then cool and peel. Return to the water and continue cooking until they are tender.

Serves 4–6 (large cock pheasants will serve 3 people generously)

Caherciveen on the Ring of Kerry

LAMB WITH CRAB-APPLE JELLY

*Crab apples can often be found for the taking, in woodland
areas and along roadsides. They are abundant in Killarney,
and their wild and winey flavour gives character to this simple
sauce. Ordinary apple jelly can be enhanced by the
addition of a little redcurrant jelly.*

1–2 racks of lamb
  (4–6 cutlets each)
3 tablespoons crab-apple jelly
3 tablespoons olive oil
a large glass each of red wine
  and stock or water
3 large garlic cloves
2–3 fresh rosemary sprigs or
  1 teaspoon dried rosemary
2 tablespoons dried pink
  peppercorns
lemon juice, if necessary
1 oz/30 g butter, chilled
  and cubed
sea salt and freshly ground
  black pepper
fresh rosemary sprigs to
  garnish

Trim the lamb of any excess fat
and neatly pare the cutlet bones.
Season with black pepper and rub
over with some of the olive oil.
Place in a deep dish and pour the
wine and stock or water over.
Crush the garlic cloves and tuck
them, with the rosemary, into the
meat. Marinate for half an hour or
so, or overnight.

  To cook, preheat the oven to
220°C/425°F/Gas Mark 7. Remove
the meat and blot dry with kitchen
paper. In a hot pan, brown the end
cutlets in the remaining oil. Rub a
little more oil over the meat and
sprinkle the skin with salt. Roast for
about 15 minutes for pink lamb,
and 5 minutes or so longer if you
prefer it nearing well done.
Remove the lamb to a dish, cover
it with foil and a towel and allow it
to rest.

  Strain the marinade into a
saucepan, add a sprig of rosemary
and the pink peppercorns (if you
can only find the brined sort, rise
off the brine and use only 1
tablespoon). Boil rapidly to reduce;
then add the crab-apple jelly,
whisking well to dissolve. Taste,
adding a little lemon if it's too
sweet. Pour any juices from the
roasting tin into the sauce, remove
the rosemary and whisk in the
butter, a piece at a time. Slice the
lamb into cutlets, 2 or 3 per
person, depending on size. Pour a
small pool of sauce on each plate
and arrange the cutlets on top.
Garnish with the rosemary sprigs.
Serves 4–6

PORK AND APPLE PIE

This pie is based on one given by Hannah Glasse in her famous 1758 cookery book,
The Art of Cookery made Plain and Easy. *This book circulated so widely
in Ireland it was said to be the only book in some houses of the day.*

2 lb/900 g good sausagemeat
  or equal quantities of pork
  pieces and pork belly, finely
  minced
4 oz/110 g streaky bacon,
  chopped finely
1¹/₂ lb/675 g apples, e.g.
  Pippins or Bramleys,
  chopped
2 large onions, peeled and
  finely chopped
1 oz/30 g butter
1 oz/30 g brown sugar
2–3 fresh sage leaves, chopped,
  or a little dried sage
5–6 juniper berries
a glass of white wine or cider
salt, freshly ground black
  pepper and grated nutmeg
1 egg, beaten, to glaze

FOR THE PASTRY
1 lb/450 g plain flour
8 oz/225 g butter
1 egg
1–2 tablespoons very cold
  water
salt, pinch

Make the pastry in the usual way
adding an egg as well as water, and
roll out two-thirds to line a
greased 9 inch/23 cm square cake
tin. Roll out the remainder to
make the lid. Chill. Preheat the
oven to 180°C/350°F/Gas Mark 4.

Sauté the onions in half the
butter until soft. Cool and add to
the sausagemeat, bacon, apples
and sugar. Season well with
pepper, a little salt and a good
grating of nutmeg. Put in the sage

(be sparing if the sage is dried).
Spread the meat in the pastry
case, pushing the juniper berries
down into the mixture. Pour over
the wine or cider and dot with
the remaining butter. If pork is
used, add a little more butter
(about 2 oz/55 g). Cover with the
pastry lid, dampening and pressing
the edges well together, and then
brush the top with the beaten
egg.

Bake for about an hour, covering
the top with foil if it's getting too
brown. Cool on a wire rack.

When cold, cut into squares and
serve with a green salad, fruity
chutney and good bread.

*Serves 4 as a main course, or 8
as a starter*

A disused shed in Co. Wexford

ROAST MICHAELMAS GOOSE WITH PRUNE, APPLE AND POTATO STUFFING

The tradition of a goose for dinner on the feast of St Michael (29th September) is as old as that of the Christmas goose, and made good sense: the spring geese were turned out to fatten among the stubble after the grain was harvested, making them comfortably plump for Michaelmas.

10-12 lb/4-5.5 kg goose
³/₄ lb/340 g prunes, soaked
  and chopped
1 lb/450 g apples, chopped
1 lb/450 g potatoes, cooked
  and mashed
1 tablespoon orange rind
1 tablespoon chopped fresh
  sage (¹/₂ teaspoon dried)
1 onion, sliced
¹/₂ oz/15 g butter
1 tablespoon sea salt
1 teaspoon caraway seeds
1 tablespoon Dijon mustard
black pepper

To drain some of the fat and dry the skin in readiness for its roasting crisply, prick the goose thoroughly all over with a fork. Pour boiling water over the skin and leave to dry in an airy place while you make the stuffing.

Cook the sliced onion in the butter until soft, then mix with the chopped prunes, apples and mashed potato. Add the caraway seeds, mustard, orange rind and herbs and season well.

When ready to cook, dry the goose skin with kitchen paper and rub well with salt. Pack the stuffing loosely into the cavity and put any surplus into a foil-covered dish to cook separately.

Secure the legs in place by passing a skewer through the first joint of one leg through to the other leg, or tie securely in place.

Sit the goose, breast side down, on a rack in a deep roasting tin and cook at 425°F/220°C/Gas 7 for 40 minutes, then lower the heat to 300°F/150°C/Gas 2, turning the goose breast side up at the half way point. Allow about 20 minutes to the pound and test by inserting a skewer between the leg and the breast; clear liquid indicates that it is done. There will be a great deal of fat, so it is more manageable to pour it off once or twice during cooking. Treasure the fat for roasting potatoes.

When the goose is ready, cover it with foil and a towel to rest for at least 30 minutes.

To make the gravy, add a little stock (made with the giblets etc.) and a glass of wine or 2 tablespoons orange juice to the de-fatted sediment in the roasting tin, scraping it up well. Boil to reduce, then whisk in a few knobs of butter.

Serve with Sautéed Cabbage (page 90).

Serves 6

A lane in Lauragh, Co. Kerry

SAUTÉED CABBAGE WITH BACON

1¹/₄ lb/560 g finely sliced or
  shredded cabbage, hard
  stalks removed
8 oz/225 g piece streaky
  bacon, cubed
2 tablespoons oil
2 tablespoons wine vinegar
6 tablespoons water
1 teaspoon sugar
1 teaspoon caraway seeds
1 large Bramley apple, peeled
  and chopped
salt and freshly ground
  black pepper

Cook the bacon cubes in the oil in
a large pan, until crisp. Remove and
keep warm. Add the vinegar, water,
sugar and caraway seeds to the
pan, scraping up the sediment, and
boil for a few moments.

Add the cabbage and apple to
the pan and cook, turning
frequently, until the cabbage is just
tender and the apple soft and
melting, about 7–8 minutes. Taste
for seasoning, sprinkle the bacon
on top and serve.

This dish is excellent with fowl
and game.

Serves 6

CHICKEN PIE WITH CASHEW NUTS

This chicken pie is ideal comfort food for cold evenings. The cashews can be replaced
by the more traditional toasted whole almonds.

4 large chicken breasts
2 chicken legs
3 oz/75 g cashew nuts
1 onion, chopped
3 carrots
8 shallots, peeled
1 bay leaf
1 ¹/₂ pints/850 ml water
2 celery sticks
1 tablespoon oil
chopped fresh or dried
**   tarragon**
2 tablespoons plain flour
2 tablespoons butter
salt, freshly ground black
**   pepper and grated nutmeg**

FOR THE TOPPING
1¹/₂ lb/675 g potatoes
1 oz/30 g butter
hot milk

Put the onion, 1 carrot and the bay leaf in the water and cook for 40 minutes, to make a stock. Strain. Cut the remaining carrots and the celery into thick slices and add, with the chicken, to the stock. Cook until the vegetables are cooked but still crisp; then remove with a slotted spoon. Remove the breasts as soon as they are just cooked, after about 12-15 minutes, and continue cooking until the legs are tender. Skin and bone the chicken legs and put the meat with the breasts. Return the trimmings to the stock and boil hard to reduce to about 1 pint/575 ml. Preheat the oven to 200°C/400°F/Gas Mark 6.

In a small pan, heat the oil and toast the nuts for a few moments; then remove and cook the shallots in the same pan, until they are nicely browned. Add a ladleful of stock and cook until they are tender. Arrange the nuts, vegetables and the chicken, which has been cut into nice pieces, in a pie dish and season well. Add a little chopped fresh tarragon, less if using dried.

Cook the flour in the melted butter in a large saucepan and then gradually add the strained hot stock, stirring well until the sauce thickens. Season well with salt, pepper and nutmeg and pour over the chicken and vegetables in the pie dish.

Boil the potatoes in their skins until tender. Mash thoroughly, adding the butter and enough hot milk to make them creamy. Spread, or pipe over the dish and cook in the top of the oven until the sauce is bubbling and the potatoes are golden brown. Follow with a salad.

Serves 4–6

Open fire in a Lixnaw cottage, north Kerry

COLCANNON

*Though variations of colcannon are eaten all year round,
it always forms part of the Hallowe'en table.
Originally the centrepiece of a meatless fast-day supper,
nowadays, it more often accompanies roasts.*

**1 lb/450 g kale or green
   cabbage**
**1¹/₂ lb/675 g potatoes,
   unpeeled**
**1 bunch scallions (spring
   onions), finely chopped**
**6 fl oz/175 ml hot cream
   or milk**
4 oz/110 g butter
salt and white pepper

Remove the hard stalks from the
kale, or cabbage, and cook in
salted, boiling water, until tender.
Kale takes a surprisingly long time,
about 25 minutes, cabbage will
take less. Drain, press out any
remaining water and chop finely.

Boil the potatoes in salted, boiling
water until soft; drain and dry over
the heat for a few minutes,
covered with a tea-towel. Peel and
mash carefully by hand, removing
any lumps, but do not use a food
processor. The scallions (spring
onions) can be cooked in the
cream or milk for a few minutes,
but I prefer them raw. Add them
to the potatoes, with the hot
cream or milk, half the butter and
the kale. Mix thoroughly together,
check and adjust the seasoning,
and put into a large serving bowl.
Make a well in the centre, which
will hold the remaining butter.
Serve very hot.

Rings, well wrapped, can be
inserted for Hallowe'en (see
Autumn introduction).
Serves 4

Bunratty Folk Park, Co. Clare

COLCANNON – A WEXFORD VERSION

Almost every region of Ireland has its version of colcannon and each claims theirs as the 'true' recipe. Like traditional dishes worldwide, the local version contains whatever is readily available. Wexford's comfortable farms were known for their vegetable gardens and orchards.

8 large potatoes, peeled
1 large parsnip, peeled, cored
1 large onion, peeled
1 cabbage or kale
4 oz/110 g butter
hot milk
a bunch of fresh parsley,
   chopped
salt and freshly ground
   black pepper
chopped fresh parsley or
   chopped scallions (spring
   onions), to garnish

Peel the potatoes. Wash, dry and chop all the vegetables in small pieces, keeping one large cabbage or kale leaf aside. Place them in a steamer or colander over hot water. Cover with the cabbage leaf and the lid and steam for 45 minutes to an hour, until all the vegetables are tender. Mash the potatoes and vegetables together, with the parsley. Season with pepper and salt and add 3 oz/75 g of butter and sufficient hot milk to make it creamy.

Serve in a mound on a deep dish with the remaining butter pressed into the centre and chopped parsley or scallions (spring onions) scattered over the top.

Serves 4

RABBIT WITH ALMONDS

Rabbit, like chicken today, was immensely popular in the past. Dozens of recipes survive from Irish household recipe books. Almonds too, were widely used for flavour and texture in a variety of dishes. Rabbit meat is extremely lean, which makes it ideal for contemporary tastes and today's tender rabbits are specially bred for the table. Wild rabbits take rather longer to cook and have a gamier flavour.

2¹/₂–3 lb/1.15–1.4 kg rabbit,
  cut into 8–10 pieces
6 oz/170 g blanched whole
  almonds
1 tablespoon vinegar
1 tablespoon salt
2 tablespoons plain flour
1 oz/30 g butter
1 tablespoon oil
2 onions, sliced
4 oz/110 g streaky bacon,
  chopped
2 tablespoons Irish whiskey
a sprig fresh thyme
1 bay leaf
a glass of white wine
a glass of stock or water
grated zest and juice of
  1 lemon
salt and freshly ground
  black pepper

Soak the rabbit for several hours in water, with the vinegar and salt. If the rabbit is wild, soak overnight.

Preheat the oven to 180°C/350°F/Gas Mark 4.

Remove from the water, rinse well and pat dry. Season the pieces and flour well. Brown the rabbit in the butter and oil in a ovenproof casserole. Add the onions and bacon and continue cooking until they soften slightly. Add the whiskey and when it has just warmed, ignite it. When the flames die down add the herbs, wine, stock or water, lemon juice and zest and almonds. Check the seasoning.

Cover tightly and transfer to the oven (it can also remain on top of the stove, if more convenient) and cook for about an hour. Test with a skewer for tenderness and add a little more wine or stock if it needs more cooking or seems to be dry.

Serve the rabbit arranged on a dish of plain boiled rice and pour the pan juices on top.

Serves 4

Roundstone Harbour, Co. Galway

BAKED COD
WITH
MUSHROOMS

4–6 cod cutlets or fillets
8¹/₂ oz/240 g mushrooms,
   diced
1 medium onion
1 leek
2 oz/55 g butter
grated zest of ¹/₂ lemon
1 dessertspoon plain flour
¹/₂ pint/280 ml hot fish stock
   or milk
6 anchovy fillets, split in half
   (optional)
1 oz/30 g breadcrumbs
salt and freshly ground
   black pepper
chopped fresh parsley, to
   garnish

Preheat the oven to
170°C/325°F/Gas Mark 3. Chop
the onion finely and slice the
cleaned leek. Cook them gently in
half the butter, until soft. Spread in
a buttered ovenproof dish and
place the seasoned fish on top.
In the same pan, melt the
remaining butter and cook the
sliced mushrooms and lemon zest
for several minutes until the juices
have run and the mushrooms are
beginning to brown. Add the flour
and stir well until the flour is
cooked, about 2–3 minutes.
Gradually add the stock or milk,
stirring well to prevent lumps from
forming. Pour the sauce over the
fish and leek mixture. If you are
using anchovies, arrange them on
top of the sauce. Sprinkle the
breadcrumbs over the top. Bake
for 25 minutes.
Serves 4–6

AUTUMN
desserts

AUTUMN APPLE TART

Armagh has been renowned for more than 200 years for the quality of her apples. This tart combines two types of apple, Bramley cooking apples for the purée, and eating apples, which hold their shape when cooked, for the apple slices. The tart can be garnished with whatever fresh fruit is in season.

FOR THE PASTRY
6 oz/170 g plain flour
1 oz/30 g caster sugar
4 oz/110 g butter
1 egg yolk
1 tablespoon lemon juice
salt

FOR THE FILLING
3 large Bramley cooking
** apples**
3 large red dessert apples
1 tablespoon grated lemon
** zest**
caster sugar to taste
1 tablespoon lemon juice
1 tablespoon melted butter
2 tablespoons icing sugar

To make the pastry, sift the flour with a pinch of salt. Stir in the sugar. Rub the butter into the flour and salt with the fingertips, or pulse in the food processor. Beat the egg yolk with the lemon juice and mix in to the pastry. Add a few drops more cold water if required. Roll out or pat into a greased 9 inch/ 23 cm tart tin. Chill for an hour.
  Preheat the oven to 190°C/375°F/Gas Mark 5. Peel and core the cooking apples and cook gently until soft, adding a spoonful of water if necessary. Press through a sieve or purée and add the grated lemon zest. Sweeten to taste with caster sugar. When cold spread over the bottom of the pastry.

Quarter and core the unpeeled red apples, cut into neat slices and brush with lemon juice. Arrange the slices in a circle around the tin, on top of the purée, covering it completely. Brush the slices with melted butter and sprinkle a little icing sugar over the top, using a nylon sieve. Cover the apple slices with a circle of foil for the first 15 minutes of cooking. Bake for about 35 minutes, until the pastry has shrunk a little from the sides of the tin and the apples are slightly tinged with colour. Serve warm or cold. Hand cream or crème fraîche separately.
  Serves 6

Near Glencar, Co. Kerry

A GREEN FOOL

The creamy unctuous qualities of the avocado are not utilised sufficiently in sweet dishes. Combined here with the last of the summer gooseberries it brings new life to the classic gooseberry fool.

1¹/₂ lb/675 g gooseberries
1 large, ripe avocado, peeled, stoned and chopped
caster sugar
grated zest and juice of a lime

Wash, top and tail the gooseberries and cook until soft. This can be done in the oven or gently on the stove but the microwave is ideal as the berries seem to keep their colour. Purée the gooseberries in a food processor and then sieve to remove the seeds. Return the purée to the processor, with the peeled and chopped avocado and blend until creamy. The avocado will discolour quickly, so sprinkle a little of the lime juice over it first. Sweeten the purée to your taste with the caster sugar, add the lime zest and the juice of half the lime. Chill for at least an hour. Serve in glasses, with pretty biscuits.
Serves 4

AUTUMN PUDDING

This is an autumnal version of summer pudding, a sort of consolation for the passing of the brilliant summer raspberries and redcurrants. In its own way, it's just as nice.
The traditional combination is apples, plums (peeled, stoned and cut into small cubes) and blackberries. The bread should be stale, at least two days old and anything from sliced pan to brioche is suitable, if it can be cut to shape. The loaf-type Barm Brack (see page 105) is excellent. Home-made custard, hot or cold, or whipped cream mixed with crème fraîche, are equally good with this.

2 lb/900 g mixed fruit,
** e.g. apples, plums,**
** blackberries, and autumn**
** rhubarb, if you like**
caster sugar to taste
8–10 stale bread slices

Cook the fruit gently in a saucepan, using as little water as possible to moisten it (1–2 tablespoons at most) or, better still, cook it in the microwave, until it is just soft and the juice is just beginning to run. Sweeten to taste.

Butter a 2 pint/1.75 litre pudding basin. Cut a round from one slice of bread to fit the bottom of the bowl, then cut the rest into sections to fit the sides, reserving some for the top. Gently spoon in the hot fruit, arrange the lid pieces to fit tightly, then cover with baking parchment or foil. Put a small plate or saucer on top and weigh it down with a tin can so that the juice will seep into the bread. Keep any juice which spills over. Allow the pudding to cool then refrigerate overnight.

To serve, run a knife around the edge between the bread and the bowl and turn out on to a deep plate. Pour any remaining juice over the top.

Serves 4 or 5

APPLE DUMPLINGS

'C– holds that a man cannot have a pure mind who refuses apple dumplings. I am not certain but he is right.'
Charles Lamb, The Essays of Elia

6 large dessert apples
1½ lb/675 g shortcrust, or
** puff pastry, home-made or**
** bought**
2 tablespoons lemon juice
5 sticks of rhubarb or
** 1 lb/450 g plums, stoned,**
** or a mixture of both**
2 tablespoons sultanas
5 oz/150 g golden granulated
** sugar**
2 oz/55 g butter
6 cloves
1 egg, beaten

Preheat the oven to 180°C/350°F/Gas Mark 4. Peel the apples and brush with lemon juice. Remove the cores and a little of the apple to enlarge the cavities. Wash and chop the rhubarb or plums, add the removed apple and the sultanas and cook gently in 1 oz/30 g of butter, until soft but not mushy (a few minutes in a microwave is ideal). Fill the apples with the fruit mixture, sweeten to taste, and add a clove to each. Top with a knob of butter.

Cut the pastry into 6 pieces and roll them out to fit the apples. Set each apple on a square of pastry and damp the edges. Draw up the corners, cut away the surplus pastry and press the edges well together, moulding to fit the apples. Roll out the pastry trimmings to make leaves and use these to cover any imperfections. Make steam holes in the top of the pastry, brush with the beaten egg and then sprinkle with sugar. Bake for about 45 minutes, until the pastry is golden brown. Very large apples may take a little longer. A skewer pressed into the side will tell if it is done.

Cooking apples can be used for apple dumplings if you like tart flavours, but add extra sugar. Vanilla ice cream is very good indeed with apple dumplings.

Serves 6

ORANGE CARAWAY CAKE

Caraway seeds, and ginger, have been intensively used in Irish cooking since at least the seventeenth century and are just as popular today. This variation on the seed, or Madeira cake is very good. Without the orange and marmalade, this recipe makes an excellent plain seed cake, which was always on hand to offer with a glass of sherry or Madeira when friends called.

4 oz/110 g butter
4 oz/110 g light brown sugar
8 oz/225 g plain flour
1¹/₄ teaspoons baking powder
2 large eggs
2 tablespoons fine cut
  marmalade
1 tablespoon caraway seeds
grated zest and juice of
  1 orange
2 tablespoons icing sugar,
  sifted
salt, pinch

Preheat the oven to 170°C/325°F/Gas Mark 3. Sift the flour with the baking powder and salt. Cream the butter and the sugar until light and fluffy and paler in colour. Add the eggs, beating them in one at a time, adding a tablespoon of flour with each. Add the marmalade, the caraway seeds and the orange zest and juice. Fold the remaining flour into the mixture. Pour into a well greased 9 inch/23 cm ring mould. Bake for about 45 minutes, until it has shrunk slightly from the sides of the tin. Cool slightly before turning out. When cold, dredge the cake with icing sugar.

CINNAMON TOAST

A tea-time treat from times past when toast was made in front of the fire. It tastes just as good today.

thick slices of white bread
butter
ground cinnamon
light brown sugar

Toast one side of the bread. Butter the untoasted side generously, sprinkle liberally with the cinnamon and then the sugar. Brown under the grill and eat immediately, while the buttery cinnamon runs down your chin.

Araglin Forest Park on the Dingle Peninsula

AUTUMN
baking

MARBLE CAKE

*Marble cake has fascinated children for generations and it is
always a popular feature of the Irish tea table.*

6 oz/170 g plain flour
1 teaspoon baking powder
salt
3 oz/75 g good dark
  chocolate or 1 tablespoon
  cocoa powder mixed with
  2 tablespoons milk
6 oz/170 g butter
6 oz/170 g caster sugar
3 large eggs
grated zest and juice of
  1 lemon

Preheat the oven to
170°C/325°F/Gas Mark 3. Sift the
flour with the baking powder and a
pinch of salt. Melt the chocolate, if
using, over hot water.

  Beat the butter in a large bowl
until soft; then add the sugar and
continue beating until the mixture
is pale and creamy. Add the eggs,
one by one, adding a spoonful of
flour with each and beating well
after each egg. Fold and cut in the

remaining flour carefully in a couple
of batches, making sure no pockets
of flour remain. Divide the mixture,
putting half into another bowl. To
this add the lemon zest and 1–2
tablespoons of juice, to your taste.
To the other bowl add the
chocolate or cocoa mixture, mixing
it in gently but thoroughly.

  Drop the mixtures into a
buttered and lined 2 lb/900 g loaf
tin, 3 spoonfuls of one and then
the other until you have used all
the mixtures. Finally, draw a knife
through the mixture diagonally
from each end of the tin to create
a marbled effect.

  Bake for 45 minutes, or until the
cake has shrunk slightly from the
sides of the tin. Cover with foil if
the top is browning too quickly.
Leave to cool briefly in the tin and
then transfer to a wire rack.

MACAROONS

These classic macaroons were an important component of the 'biscuit tin', to be offered with a glass of sherry or a cup of tea.

4 oz/110 g ground almonds
almond or ratafia essence
8 oz/225 g caster sugar
1 oz/30 g rice flour
2 large egg whites
rice paper
flaked almonds

Preheat the oven to 180°C/350°F/Gas Mark 4. Line a buttered baking tray with rice paper. Lightly whisk the egg whites with a fork.

Mix the ground almonds, essence, sugar and rice flour together. Mix in the whites thoroughly. Using a teaspoon, drop spoonfuls of the mixture on to the rice paper, well apart. Top each with an almond flake and bake until golden brown, about 8–10 minutes. Remove, still on the rice paper, to a rack to cool. Tear or cut away the excess paper from the edges of the biscuits. The rice paper is, of course, edible.
Makes about 20

Caherconree, Iveragh Peninsula

Walnut Cake

10 oz/275 g plain flour
3¹/₂ oz/100 g walnuts
7 oz/200 g butter, at room
   temperature
6 oz/170 g caster sugar
4 large eggs, at room
   temperature
1 teaspoon vanilla essence
grated zest and juice of a
   lemon

Preheat the oven to
180°C/350°F/Gas Mark 4 and
butter and line a 2 lb/900 g loaf tin.
Sift the flour. Crumble the walnuts
with your fingers.

In a large bowl cream the butter.
Then add the sugar, beating until
pale and creamy. Add the eggs, one
by one, adding a tablespoon of
flour and beating between each.

Mix in the walnuts, vanilla and a
tablespoon of lemon juice. Beat
them in well and then fold in the
remaining flour, in 3 parts, cutting it
in rather than beating it, but making
sure no flour pockets remain.
Transfer the mixture to the
prepared tin and sprinkle the top
with lemon zest. Place a piece of
foil loosely over the top and bake
for about an hour, lowering the
heat to 170°C/325°F/Gas Mark 3
and removing the foil after half an
hour. Bake 45 minutes until the
cake shrinks slightly from the sides
of the tin. When cooked, cool for a
few minutes in the tin before
removing to a wire rack.

The cake can be iced with a little
icing sugar, mixed with a
tablespoon of lemon juice and
spread over the top. It will keep for
a few days in a tin.

The walnuts can be toasted for 5
minutes in the oven for a nuttier
flavour, but watch carefully as they
burn quickly.

BARM BRACK

The barm brack (barm is the yeasty ferment produced when brewing ale or beer; brack, or breac, refers to its speckled nature) is one of the few Irish traditional breads or cakes raised with yeast, and, like hot cross buns, the origins are lost in antiquity. It is an essential part of the Hallowe'en festivities and usually contains a ring – whoever gets the ring will be married within the year.

12 oz/340 g mixed dried fruit
  and candied peel
1¹/₄ lb/560 g plain white
  flour
4–5 saffron strands
2 tablespoons water
1 teaspoon salt
2 oz/55 g brown sugar
2 teaspoons ground mixed
  spice, or to taste
1 sachet of easy-blend dried
  yeast
3 oz/75 g butter
2 eggs, beaten
¹/₂ pint/280 ml warm milk

TO GLAZE
1 tablespoon sugar
4 tablespoons water

Put the saffron to soak in two tablespoons of water for 15 minutes. In a large bowl mix the flour, salt, sugar, spice and dried yeast together. Rub in the butter and then add the fruit and peel. Add the beaten eggs and the saffron mixture to the warm milk. Make a well in the flour mixture and pour in the liquid, reserving a tablespoon. Mix well together,

drawing in the flour from the sides. When the mixture will hold together, turn out and knead for 5–6 minutes. Return to the bowl and cover with cling film. Allow to rise for about an hour in a warm place.

Grease two 8 inch/20 cm cake tins 3 inch/7.5 cm deep and, if you like, wrap two inexpensive rings in greaseproof paper. Turn the dough out and knead again briefly, then divide between the cake tins. Press the rings into the centre and allow to rise for a further 30 minutes.

Preheat the oven to 220°C/425°F/Gas Mark 7. Brush the cakes with the reserved liquid and bake for about 10 minutes; then reduce heat to 190°C/375°F/Gas Mark 5 and bake until a hollow sound results when the bottom is tapped, about 40–50 minutes. Make a glaze with the tablespoon of sugar and the water, boiled together until reduced. Brush over the bracks and return to the oven to set for 5 minutes.

Lough Delphi, Co. Mayo. Overleaf: Brandon Mountain, Co. Kerry

WINTER

WITH Hallowe'en past and the gardens tidied up and put to bed, the focus turns to Christmas. The preparation of cakes and puddings usually began in November and it was the custom for everyone living in the house to stir the pudding for luck.

This was an invariable rule in my own home and there was a vague dread in our minds, as children, that if everyone didn't stir it something might happen to the pudding: a disaster, since it was the thing we liked best for the Christmas feast.

Christmas is still an intensely family affair in Ireland and the prospect of children home from school and perhaps friends or family home from abroad brings an air of excitement to the preparations. Turkey is the most popular centrepiece of the Christmas dinner, although many people still prefer goose, and there is always a splendid ham to partner the turkey, and spiced beef to hand around with drinks. On Christmas Eve, candles are still lighted in the windows to welcome the Holy Family and guide them to rest. The Feast of the Epiphany, 6th January, is known in Ireland as Little Christmas or Nollaig na mBan, Women's Christmas, when women had their own feast with all the dishes dear to their hearts. This excellent custom, though rather in abeyance for some years, is now happily enjoying a revival.

OYSTERS IN CHAMPAGNE SAUCE

The charm of this dish lies in the combination of the hot sauce with the cold oysters, the perfect introduction to the Christmas dinner. The sauce can be made in advance and reheated.

24 oysters
a glass of champagne or
   white wine
3 shallots, very finely
   chopped
1 oz/30 g butter
1¹/₂ tablespoons plain flour
¹/₂ pint/280 ml cream
cayenne pepper or Tabasco
   sauce
chopped fresh parsley, to
   garnish

Scrub the oysters thoroughly and soak them for an hour or so in cold water.

Open the oysters carefully (see below), saving as much of their liquid as possible, and put them to chill while you make the sauce.

Cook the shallots in a pan, with the butter, until transparent but not brown.

Add the flour and stir well until it is cooked. Add the champagne or wine and the strained oyster liquid to the roux, whisking well to prevent lumps and cooking until reduced somewhat, about 5 or 6 minutes. Gradually add the cream and simmer for a few moments. Simmer gently until the sauce has reduced and thickened sufficiently. Season to your taste with the cayenne or Tabasco – it probably won't need salt. Use paprika if cayenne is too hot.

When you are ready to serve, arrange the oysters on plates and put a spoonful of the hot sauce over each cold oyster. Garnish with parsley.

Note: to open an oyster, hold it firmly in your left hand and insert a short sharp knife near the hinge, working it from right to left until the muscle is severed; then prise the oyster open.

Serves 4

Gathering seaweed, Brandon Bay, Co. Kerry. Previous pages: Conor Pass, Co. Kerry.

SMOKED FISH TART WITH ARDRAHAN CHEESE

Combining Ardrahan cheese, from Kanturk, Co. Cork, with smoked fish, is the inspirational idea of Geert Maes, chef patron of Gaby's Restaurant in Killarney, one of Ireland's most respected restaurants. It is partnered here with smoked haddock, to make a simple but delicious tart.

FOR THE PASTRY

4 oz/110 g butter

7 oz/200 g plain flour

$^1/_4$ teaspoon salt

1 egg yolk

1–2 tablespoons very cold
water, if necessary

FOR THE FILLING

8 oz/225 g smoked haddock
or cod

4 oz/110 g Ardrahan cheese

1 onion, chopped

1 carrot, chopped

$^1/_2$ tablespoon oil

1 bay leaf

4 large eggs

$^1/_2$ pint/280 ml cream

freshly ground black pepper
and grated nutmeg

Preheat the oven to 200°C/400°F/Gas Mark 6. To make the pastry, rub the butter into the sifted flour and salt, moisten with the egg yolk, adding a tablespoon or so of cold water if required. Roll out, or press into a 9 x 2 inch//23 x 5 cm quiche tin. Chill until required.

Soften the chopped onion and carrot in the oil, add the bay leaf and pepper and enough water just to cover. Boil for about 10 minutes. Gently poach the fish in this stock until cooked, 5–6 minutes. Take out the fish, flake and remove any bones or hard pieces. Keep the stock for soups.

With a potato peeler, remove the thin outer rind from the Ardrahan cheese and then cut the cheese into thin slices. Arrange these on the base of the pastry and put the flaked fish on top.

Beat the cream and eggs together and season well with black pepper and a pinch of nutmeg. It probably won't need salt. Pour into the pastry and bake for about 40 minutes until golden on top and the pastry has shrunk slightly away from the sides of the tin. Reduce the oven to 50°C/ 300°F/Gas Mark 2 after 5 minutes.

Serves 4 as a main course,
6 as a starter

Kinvara village, Co. Galway

WALNUT SOUP WITH WALNUT AND CRESS SANDWICHES

This simple soup is best made in the winter, when the new season's nuts are fresh. Good home-made stock will also greatly add to the flavour. This soup is particularly popular with men – perhaps because it was frequently served in conjunction with game.

4 oz/110 g shelled walnuts
1 large garlic clove
1¼ pints/675 ml chicken
   stock
½ pint/280 ml cream
grated nutmeg
salt and freshly ground
   black pepper
1 tablespoon finely chopped
fresh chives or parsley, to
   garnish

FOR THE SANDWICH FILLING
4 oz/110 g cream cheese
2 tablespoons of finely
   chopped walnuts
2–3 tablespoons of chopped
   cress

To make the soup, crush or blend the walnuts and garlic to a smooth paste, adding a little stock to help it along. Blend in the rest of the stock, add the cream and season well, grating a very little nutmeg over it. Bring to the boil and simmer gently for 4–6 minutes before serving. Garnish with the herbs.

To make the sandwich filling, beat together the cream cheese, walnuts and cress.

Serves 4

BAKED EGGS
WITH SPINACH

**4 large eggs, at room
   temperature
8 oz/225 g spinach
2 streaky bacon rashers
$^{1}/_{4}$ pint/150 ml cream
1 tablespoon butter
soy sauce
black pepper and salt
chopped fresh chervil**

Preheat the oven to
180°C/350°F/Gas Mark 4. Wash
the spinach and remove the
stalks. Chop coarsely, place in a
pan with a knob of butter and
stew gently until just tender.
Squeeze out the moisture.

Cook the bacon until crisp and
then chop finely.

Butter 4 ramekins. Put a
tablespoon of spinach in each,
sprinkle the bacon over it and
season well, adding a drop or two
of soy sauce to each dish. Crack
the eggs into the dishes and
cover with the cream. Sprinkle
the chervil over the top. Bake for
about 12–15 minutes, until the
egg whites are set and the yolks
still soft.

Serves 4 as a starter

CELERY SOUP WITH BLUE CHEESE

1 large head of celery
2–3 oz/55–75 g Chetwynde
  blue cheese, crumbled
2 garlic cloves
1 onion
2 pints/1.1 litres vegetable or
  light chicken stock
$^{1}/_{4}$ pint/150 ml cream
1 oz/30 g butter
1 oz/30 g plain flour
2–3 scallions (spring onions),
finely chopped, to garnish

Prepare and finely chop the celery, garlic and onion and cook in the butter, in a large saucepan, stirring frequently, until the vegetables begin to soften. Sift in the flour and stir well until it has cooked. Gradually add the hot stock, mixing well to avoid lumps. Cook for 10 minutes or so, until the vegetables are completely cooked, and then put through the blender.

Return the soup to the saucepan, season well and add the cream. (If it seems too thick, add a little milk also.) Cook for a few moments to amalgamate the cream. Just before serving, bring back to the boil and stir in the crumbled cheese, but don't continue to boil once it has been added.

Garnish with the finely chopped scallions (spring onions). Serve with crusty bread.

Serves 6

Gleann na Gealt (Valley of the Mad Men), Co. Kerry

RAGOUT OF COD AND CLAMS

In the past, clams made only very occasional appearances on our western shores, but in recent years they have been cultivated very successfully and have found a natural place in Irish cooking. Basmati rice or new potatoes, buttered and sprinkled with herbs, are good served with this.

1¹/₂ lb/675 g cod
1¹/₂ lb/675 g clams
2 large onions
1 tablespoon olive oil
2 garlic cloves
3 tablespoons balsamic
    vinegar
¹/₂ pint/280 ml fish or
    chicken stock
2 tins of chopped Italian
    tomatoes
1 tablespoon chopped fresh
    coriander
salt and freshly ground
    black pepper

Slice the onions into fine rings and put them in a heavy, flameproof casserole or saucepan, with the oil and garlic. Sauté gently until they are soft but not brown; then add the balsamic vinegar and the stock. Cover and cook over a moderate heat until the stock has almost evaporated and become slightly syrupy, but watch it so that it doesn't burn. This takes about 10–15 minutes. Now add the tomatoes and coriander and cook for another 10 minutes, to reduce slightly.

Taste for seasoning; it may not need salt.

Cut the cod in large cubes and add, with the clams, still in their shells, to the sauce. Cover and cook gently for 6–7 minutes until the cod is cooked and the clams have opened. Discard any clams which are still closed. Add a few grinds of black pepper and serve.

Serves 6, as a main course

Roundstone Harbour and the Twelve Pins, Co. Galway

SPICED BEEF

Spiced beef is one of the seasonal pleasures of Christmas. Decorated with holly and embalmed in spice, it can be seen in every butcher's shop during the Christmas season. To make at home, you must start a week or ten days before it is required.

TO PREPARE

4–5 lb/1.8–2.2 kg round of
  beef, bone removed
$^1/_4$ oz/7 g saltpetre
10 oz/275 g salt
5 oz/140 g brown sugar
4 oz/110 g ground mixed
spice, including mace and
  nutmeg
2 tablespoons juniper berries,
  slightly crushed

TO COOK

2 onions, roughly chopped
2 carrots, roughly chopped
2 celery sticks, roughly
  chopped
2 bay leaves

Mix all the ingredients together and rub thoroughly into the meat, making sure the bone cavity is well treated. Put the meat in a deep bowl in the refrigerator, and turn it each day, basting well with the liquid which seeps out. After ten days, it is ready for cooking. Place the vegetables and bay leaves in a large saucepan and lay the meat on top. Just cover with cold water, bring slowly to the boil and simmer gently, allowing about 25 minutes per lb/450 g. When cooked, allow the meat to rest in the water for 30 minutes. Remove to a board. If it is to be eaten cold, usually the case at Christmas, lay another board on top and press overnight with a weight.

Serve cut in very thin slices, with mustard, creamed horseradish and chutney.

Note: saltpetre can be obtained from the chemist/drugstore. It is not essential; it is used to give colour to the meat.

*Serves 8 as a main course,
10–12 as part of a buffet*

VENISON PASTIES

These small pasties are a manageable version of the great decorated venison pies of the past.
These were 'side board' dishes which allowed the pastry cooks to show off their art.
Widely available, both farmed and wild, during the winter, venison is a lean meat and benefits
from a pre-cooking marinade, which should be as long as time allows.

2 lb/900 g breast of venison,
  or pieces
2 large onions
1 carrot
1 celery stick
4 oz/110 g piece of fat bacon
2 tablespoons red-wine
  vinegar
2 tablespoons olive oil
1 glass red wine
2 lb/900 g puff pastry
1 egg, beaten
freshly ground black pepper
ground mace
salt
2 cloves garlic, crushed
6–7 juniper berries, slightly
  crushed

Cut the venison into cubes and put them in an ovenproof dish, with the oil, vinegar, crushed garlic, wine and spices to taste.

Leave overnight, if possible.
   Preheat the oven to 170°C/325°F/Gas Mark 3. Chop the vegetables finely. Cut the bacon into small cubes and fry until crisp. Add the bacon and vegetables to the meat and marinade, cover and bake for 45 minutes to an hour, or until the meat is just tender. Venison does not benefit from overcooking. Remove and cool.
   Turn the oven up to 180°C/350°F/Gas Mark 4. Roll the pastry out to make 6 pieces 6 x 8 inch/15 x 20 cm, patching together if necessary. Pour off and keep any excess gravy from the meat filling. Divide the filling between the pastry pieces, putting it in the centre and leaving a gap of 2 inches/ 5 cm on either side and

1 inch/2.5 cm at the top and bottom. Damp the edges with beaten egg and draw the sides together, pinching well. Pinch together the tops and bottoms securely. Lay the pasties on a baking-parchment-lined baking tray, seam-side down, and make a hole in the top. Brush over with beaten egg, decorate as lavishly as the pastry trimmings will allow, and bake at 180°C/350°F/Gas Mark 4 until the pastry is golden brown, about 40-45 minutes.
   The remaining gravy can be reheated and handed round separately, with a dash of lemon juice added. Rowanberry or redcurrant jelly is very good with venison.
   Serves 6

Stooking turf on the Glenbeigh Road, Co. Kerry

BEEF AND MUSHROOM PIE WITH GUINNESS

Leg of beef is a good choice for dishes of this type, for, although it takes a long time to cook initially, it remains tender and juicy.

2 lb/900 g leg or shin of
  beef, cubed and trimmed
³/₄ pint/450 ml Guinness
8 oz/225 g mushrooms
2 tablespoons plain flour
2 tablespoons olive oil
2 large onions, chopped
1 carrot, chopped
1 celery stick, chopped
bouquet garni of 1 bay leaf,
  1 fresh thyme sprig and
  1 fresh parsley sprig, tied
  with string
4 tinned anchovies, drained
8 oz/225 g puff pastry
1 egg, beaten
salt and freshly ground
  black pepper

Toss the beef in the flour and brown in the oil in a large saucepan. Add the onions, carrot, celery, the bouquet garni and seasoning. Mash the anchovies and stir in. Pour the Guinness over the top, stir well, cover and cook very gently until the meat is almost tender, about 1½ hours. (This can be done in the oven, if preferred.)

Add the mushrooms and continue cooking for another 25 minutes. Allow to cool.

Preheat the oven to 190°C/375°F/Gas Mark 5. Transfer the contents of the saucepan to a deep pie dish and check the seasoning.

Roll the pastry out on a floured board, until you have a large circle about 1½ inches/4 cm larger than the pie dish. Cut the surplus off in a long strip and press on to the dampened edge of the dish. Lay the remaining pastry circle over the pie, pressing on to the strip to attach it well and crimping the edges decoratively. Make a vent in the centre and decorate the pie with leaves or flowers made from the pastry trimmings. Brush with the beaten egg and bake until the pastry is risen and golden.

Serve with really creamy mashed potatoes, made with plenty of butter and milk and dusted over with parsley. Follow with a green salad.

Serves 6

Ballyduff potato pickers, Co. Kerry

STUFFED PORK CHOPS WITH POTATO APPLE FRITTERS

**4 loin chops, 1 inch/
  2.5 cm thick
1 tablespoon balsamic
  vinegar
grated zest and juice of
  1 lemon
1 tablespoon Dijon mustard
chopped fresh parsley
2 oz/55 g brown
  breadcrumbs
finely chopped fresh thyme
1$^{1}/_{2}$ oz/40 g butter
1 tablespoon grated fresh
  root ginger
1 apple, Cox's pippin, or
  similar, finely chopped
1 egg, beaten
$^{1}/_{4}$ pint/150 ml cider, white
  wine or chicken stock
1 tablespoon oil
salt and freshly ground
  black pepper**

**FOR THE FRITTERS
8 oz/225 g raw potato, grated
4 oz/110 g apple, grated
2 oz/55 g plain flour
2 eggs
2 tablespoons cream
oil and butter, for frying
salt**

Make cuts in the fat along the edge of the chops at $^{1}/_{2}$ inch/1 cm intervals (this helps the fat to cook and prevents the chops from curling up when heated). Make a horizontal incision in the side of each chop, to form a pocket. Mix the vinegar, lemon juice and mustard together and toss the meat well in this mixture.

Leave to marinate while you make the stuffing, or longer, if time allows.

Put the parsley in a bowl with the lemon zest, breadcrumbs and thyme. Melt $^{1}/_{2}$ oz/15 g of butter in a large pan and cook the ginger for a few moments, then add the apple and cook until soft. Mix in the breadcrumbs, season well and bind with the beaten egg. Spoon the stuffing into the pockets in the chops and secure with cocktail sticks or poultry pins.

Add half the remaining butter and the oil to the pan and, turning up the heat, brown the chops well on either side. Add the cider, wine or stock and the remaining marinade. Cover the pan, lower the heat and cook very gently until the chops are done – 10–12 minutes. Remove the chops to a serving dish and keep warm. Add the remaining butter to the pan, scrape up the residue, bubble for a few moments to reduce, check and adjust the seasoning, and pour over the chops. Keep the chops warm while you make the fritters.

Mix the potato and apples together with the flour. Bind with the eggs and cream and mix to a batter consistency. Fry, a tablespoon at a time, in hot oil and butter; drain and sprinkle with salt.

Serves 4

Dingle Bay, Co. Kerry

BREAST OF CHICKEN
WITH WALNUT AND APPLE

On rainy days alone I dine,
Upon a chick, and pint of wine.
On rainy days I dine alone,
And pick my chicken to the bone.
Jonathan Swift

4 large chicken breasts
3 oz/75 g walnuts, chopped
¹/₂ large Bramley (cooking)
   apple, peeled and chopped
2 oz/55 g butter
4 fresh sage leaves, finely
   chopped, or a tiny pinch of
   dried sage
2 tablespoons plain flour
1 egg, beaten
3 oz/75 g breadcrumbs
1 tablespoon oil
¹/₄ pint/150 ml double cream
   or crème fraîche
paprika, salt and freshly
   ground black pepper

In a small pan, melt ¹/₂ oz/15 g of butter and add the peeled and chopped apple, the sage and the walnuts. Cook gently until the apple is just beginning to soften and the walnuts beginning to colour. Set aside to cool and season well.

Make a long, deep incision in the sides of the chicken breasts, cutting lengthways to make a deep pocket. Divide the stuffing between the chicken breasts, pushing it well into the pockets. Season and flour the chicken and then dip in egg and roll in breadcrumbs. Seal with cocktail sticks. (If the chicken is being prepared in advance, chill the stuffing before inserting it.)

In a large pan, melt 1 oz/30 g of butter with the oil and fry the chicken gently, turning once or twice, until cooked and golden, but still moist, about 5–7 minutes on each side, depending on thickness.

Remove the chicken and keep warm. Wipe any burnt crumbs from the pan with kitchen paper and pour in the cream. Add any remaining stuffing or crumbs, season well with salt, pepper and paprika and bubble up for a few moments, scraping up the sediment; whisk in the remaining butter and pour over the chicken.
   Serves 4

ROAST TURKEY

This traditional turkey has two stuffings and is semi-braised, to retain moisture.

12 lb/5.5 kg turkey

2 oz/50 g butter

2 large onions, halved

8 cloves

2 carrots, coarsely chopped

2 celery sticks, coarsely
   chopped

8 oz/225 g bacon, cut in
   strips

1/2 pint/280 ml cider or
   white wine

salt and freshly ground
   black pepper

**FOR THE PRUNE AND
CHICKEN LIVER STUFFING**

8 oz/225 g prunes, stoned
and chopped

8 oz/225 g chicken livers,
cleaned and chopped

12 oz/340 g fresh
   breadcrumbs

1 large onion, finely chopped

2 oz /55 g butter

1 celery stick, finely chopped

1 carrot, grated

a small glass of vermouth or
   sherry

2 teaspoons dried mixed
   herbs

1 teaspoon ground mace

salt and freshly ground
   black pepper

**FOR THE APPLE AND
WALNUT STUFFING**

6 oz/170 g walnuts, chopped

2 cooking apples, peeled and
   chopped

2 oz/55 g butter, softened

1 tablespoon grated fresh
   root ginger

2 oz/55 g fresh breadcrumbs

salt and freshly ground
   black pepper

Preheat the oven to
230°C/450°F/Gas Mark 8. To
make the prune stuffing, cook the
onion in half the butter; then add
the livers and cook until slightly
pink. Add to the breadcrumbs. In
the remaining butter, cook the
celery, carrot and prunes for a
few minutes; then add the
vermouth or sherry, the herbs
and mace. Season to taste. Bubble
up well. Pour into the
breadcrumb mixture and mix
well. Allow to cool.

To make the apple stuffing, mix
all the ingredients together and
season well. Stuff the turkey's
body cavity loosely with the
prune stuffing. Insert slices of
butter under the breast skin.
Skewer or tie the legs together.
Stuff the crop with the apple
stuffing and seal with a skewer.
Season the turkey thoroughly and
rub the breast well with butter.

Put the halved onions, stuck
with the cloves, in a deep roasting
pan with the vegetables, bacon
and cider. Lay the turkey on its
side on top.

Put the turkey in the oven and
immediately lower the heat to
180°C/350°F/Gas Mark 4. After
45 minutes, turn the turkey on to
the other side and baste well.
After a further 45 minutes, turn
the turkey breast-side up and
continue cooking for a further 45

minutes to an hour, basting well
and covering the breast with foil if
it is browning too fast. Test by
inserting a skewer between the
thigh and the breast; the juices
should be clear. Remove the
turkey to a dish and cover with
foil and a towel; leave to relax the
meat and keep it juicy. It will stay
warm for 45 minutes to an hour.

To make the gravy, strain off the
stock from the roasting tin and
leave it to stand so the fat rises to
the top. Remove the fat and set it
aside. Mix 1 tablespoon of flour
with 1 tablespoon of the fat in a
saucepan and blend in the stock.
Boil hard to thicken slightly and
reduce. Pour into a sauceboat
and serve very hot.

Crisp bacon rolls and sausages
can be used to garnish the dish
and rowanberry jelly can be
handed separately. The prune
stuffing can be baked separately if
preferred.

Serves 8-10

Conor Pass, Co. Kerry

savouring Ireland **125**

GRATIN OF PARSNIPS AND PEARS

'Fair words butter no parsnips'
Old saying.
This is a simple and delicious recipe which can be prepared in advance and finished when required.

3–4 large parsnips
3 large pears
2 oz/55 g butter
1 tablespoon lemon juice
1 oz/30 g stale breadcrumbs
salt and freshly ground
   black pepper
grated nutmeg

Preheat the oven to 180°C/350°F/Gas Mark 4. Cut the parsnips in quarters lengthways and cut away some of the hard core, then peel, trim and cut into chunks. Peel and core the pears and chop roughly.

Put the parsnips and pears in a large saucepan. Add salt and lemon juice and just barely cover with water. Boil gently until tender. Drain well and mash with the butter until creamy, adding pepper to taste and a grating of nutmeg.

Transfer to an oven dish and sprinkle the breadcrumbs over the top. Bake for 15- 20 minutes or until golden brown.

Serves 6

ORANGE, CELERY AND WATERCRESS SALAD

This winter salad is the classic partner for wild duck. It is equally good with tame fowl, and pork. Lamb's lettuce or rocket, in season, can also be used.

2–3 oranges
6–8 celery sticks, finely sliced
1–2 bunches of watercress
1 small onion, finely chopped
2 tablespoons olive oil
1 tablespoon lemon juice
salt and paprika

Peel the oranges, removing as much pith as possible. Wash and gently shake the watercress dry. Arrange on a flat dish, with the celery. Slice the oranges thinly and arrange on top, removing any pips.

Sprinkle the finely chopped onion over the oranges and season with salt. Dress the salad with oil and lemon only when ready to serve and sprinkle a little paprika over the top.

Serves 6

Cloghane on the Dingle Peninsula

CHRISTMAS CHUTNEY

2 lb/900 g Bramley apples
12 oz/340 g onions, finely
  chopped
¹/₂ pint/280 ml white-wine
  or malt vinegar
8 oz/225 g white sugar
3 oz/75 g brown sugar
8 oz/225 g mixed nuts, e.g.
  chestnuts, walnuts and
  almonds
2 teaspoons ground ginger
grated zest and juice of
  1 lemon
1 teaspoon salt

Peel, core and chop the apples.
Cook the onions in the vinegar,
until soft. Add the apples, cook
for 3–4 minutes, and then add
the remaining ingredients and
simmer gently, until the mixture
begins to thicken, lowering the
heat and stirring frequently to
prevent it from burning.
Pot into warm, sterilised jars that
have plastic-lined lids.
Chutneys improve with keeping,
the flavours becoming more
subtle after about 2–3 months. If
the chutney is made for
immediate use, wine vinegar is
best, because malt vinegar needs
time to mellow.
  Makes about 5 x 12 oz/
335 g jars

A warm corner

ROWANBERRY JELLY

The rowan tree, or mountain ash, like the elder tree, had important magical properties for our Celtic ancestors. The red berries make an excellent jelly for game, hams and pâtés, the flavour maturing as it ages. Rowanberry jelly can be used instead of redcurrant jelly, in sauces and with lamb.

3 lb/1.4 kg rowanberries
2 large Bramleys or other cooking apples, coarsely chopped
grated zest and juice of 1 lemon
sugar

Put the rowanberries in a large saucepan and crush them slightly. Add the coarsely chopped apples (no need to peel or core) and lemon zest. Just cover with water and cook until both are very soft. Strain overnight, through a jelly bag. An old linen tea-towel over a large plastic colander can be used.

Measure the juice collected, add the lemon juice, and allow 1 lb/450 g of sugar to 1 pint/ 575 ml of liquid and boil hard until a few drops on a chilled saucer will wrinkle when pressed with a finger. Pot into hot, sterilised jars.

Makes 6 x 12 oz/335 g jars

LONGFORD CAKES

These delicious mouthfuls are simple to make for afternoon tea. Made larger, in 4 inch/10 cm tart tins, they make a very good dessert.

FOR THE PASTRY
10 oz/275 g plain flour, sifted
6 oz/170 g butter
1 tablespoon caster sugar
2 egg yolks
1–2 tablespoons cold water
salt

FOR THE FILLING
2 tablespoons ground
   almonds
5 tablespoons apricot jam
3¹/₂ oz/100 g walnuts,
   chopped coarsely
5 tablespoons sultanas
2 tablespoons very finely
   chopped apple
1 tablespoon grated
   lemon zest
1 egg, beaten, to glaze
sugar, to decorate

FOR THE GERANIUM CREAM
2–3 scented geranium leaves
8 fl oz/225 ml double or
   whipping cream

To make the pastry, mix together the flour, sugar and a pinch of salt. Rub in the butter, and then moisten with the egg yolks, adding a tablespoon or so of cold water as required. Chill for 30 minutes.

   Preheat the oven to 190°C/375°F/Gas Mark 5. If making the larger version, grease and line six 4 inch/10 cm tartlet tins; for smaller cakes use well buttered patty tins. Roll out the pastry very thinly and line the tins, gathering the trimmings and re-rolling to make the lids. Mix all the filling ingredients together, chopping finely any large pieces of apricot in the jam, and divide between the tarts. Dampen the pastry edges and put on the lids, press well together to seal and tidy up the edges. Glaze with the beaten egg, make vents in the tops and sprinkle with sugar. Bake for 25–30 minutes, until the pastry is golden brown, 5 minutes more for the larger size.

   Serve with geranium cream, which can be made as follows: wash and dry the scented geranium leaves. Softly whip the cream. Infuse the leaves in the cream for several hours.

   Makes 6 large or 12 small tarts

A BOWL OF BISHOP

This was the favourite 'night-cap' of the eighteenth century, famed in song and verse. Jonathan Swift wrote about it, though when Stella made it for him, the oranges were roasted in front of the fire, and the wine heated with a hot poker.

4 oranges
20 cloves
1 cinnamon stick
2–3 pieces of mace
1 teaspoon allspice berries
1 pint/580 ml water
a bottle of ruby port
sugar lumps or caster sugar
1 nutmeg
juice of 1 lemon

Preheat the oven to 180°C/350°F/Gas Mark 4. Make incisions in 2 of the oranges, press the cloves into them and roast for half an hour or so, until they make a slightly hissing sound.

Put the whole spices in the water in a saucepan (if you can't get whole mace, use a nutmeg or more allspice berries) and boil until reduced by half. In another saucepan, heat the port gently; then ignite it to burn off some of the alcohol and concentrate the flavour. (If you can't bear to do this, ignore it!)

Put the port, spice water and roasted oranges into a large bowl, ideally one which can be kept warm, and add sugar to taste. Slice the remaining oranges into the bowl, grate in some nutmeg and sharpen the flavour with lemon juice.

Makes about 8 glasses

Longford cakes and a bowl of bishop

CHRISTMAS PUDDING

While today's taste is for lighter food, an exception is always made in favour of the traditional Christmas pudding, although it, too, is evolving – butter is widely used today instead of suet and there hasn't been any meat in it for almost a hundred years.

8 oz/225 g each raisins,
   currants and sultanas
6 oz/170 g glacé cherries
8 oz/225 g candied peel
3 oz/75 g each walnuts and
   blanched almonds
12 oz/340 g breadcrumbs
2 oz/55 g plain flour
8 oz/225 g light brown sugar
1 large apple, peeled and
   chopped
3 teaspoons ground,
   mixed spice
12 oz/340 g butter or
   shredded suet
8 eggs
a large glass of Irish whiskey
   or sherry
6 fl oz/175 ml Guinness
salt

Cut the cherries in half. Thinly slice the peel and then chop it finely. Chop the nuts coarsely. Mix all the fruit together with the breadcrumbs, flour, sugar, apple, dried fruit, spices and a pinch of salt. Add the suet, if it is being used.

Soften the butter, if using, and gradually beat the eggs into it, with the whiskey or sherry. Pour this mixture into the dry ingredients and mix well. Add enough of the Guinness to give a dropping texture but don't make it too runny.

Place discs of baking parchment in the bottoms of two 1½ pint/850 ml pudding basins and butter them well. Fill the bowls two-thirds full, to leave room for expansion. Cover the tops with more buttered paper and then cover well with foil. The

puddings will take 5–6 hours steaming. They can also be cooked at a low heat in the oven, by standing the bowls in a tin of water and enclosing both tin and bowl completely in foil, making a sort of steam-proof tent, for 5½ hours at 150°C/300°F/ Gas Mark 2.

When cooked, allow to cool before removing the foil. Cover with fresh baking parchment and more foil before storing in a cool place until required. The puddings will require a further steaming of 1½–2 hours, before they are eaten.

Note: the puddings can be left overnight in the refrigerator before cooking, if it's not convenient to cook them immediately.

Each pudding serves 6

PEARS POACHED IN WHITE WINE

6 pears
a bottle of sweet white wine,
  e.g. Muscatel or similar
4 oz/110 g caster sugar
2 cinnamon sticks
grated zest of 1 small orange
1 tablespoon lemon juice
grated nutmeg, to decorate

Put the sugar, cinnamon sticks, orange zest and wine in a saucepan which will just hold the pears upright. Heat the liquid gently until the sugar is dissolved, and then boil hard for a few minutes.

Peel the pears carefully, leaving the stalks on and brushing each with lemon juice. Trim the bottoms slightly, so they will stand upright. Poach in the wine for about 15 minutes, or until they are tender but not too soft. If there is insufficient liquid to come up to the stalks, add water.

When the pears are cooked, remove and cool. Take the cinnamon sticks out of the poaching liquid and boil the liquid hard, uncovered, until it forms a thin syrup. Leave to cool. Pour the syrup over the pears and grate a little nutmeg over the top before serving.

Serves 6

Sunset on the Dingle Peninsula

COFFEE WALNUT ICE CREAM

$^1/_2$ **pint/280 ml milk**
5 tablespoons freshly ground coffee
1 pint/575 ml cream
7 egg yolks
6 oz/170 g caster sugar
2 tablespoons rum
3$^1/_2$ oz/100 g walnuts

Bring the milk to the boil, stir in the coffee and allow to infuse for 30 minutes. Strain the milk and stir the cream into it. Beat the egg yolks and sugar together, until pale and creamy. Gradually beat in the milk. Return to the saucepan and cook gently until the mixture thickens slightly and will coat the back of a spoon. Do not allow to boil. Allow to cool.

Chop the walnuts finely and mix into the custard, with the rum. Freeze in the usual manner by taking the mixture out and beating well 2–3 times during freezing, to prevent the formation of ice particles.

Serve in glasses with Cats' Tongues or similar little biscuits.
Serves 4–6

CATS' TONGUES

3 oz/75 g butter
3 oz/75 g caster sugar
3 egg whites
3 oz/75 g plain flour, sifted

Preheat the oven to 200°C/400°F/Gas Mark 6. Cream the butter and sugar together, until pale and creamy. Add the unbeaten egg whites. Mix well, and then gradually fold in the flour.

Line 2 trays with baking parchment and pipe the mixture into little strips 2 inches/5 cm long and about $^1/_4$ inch/5 mm wide. Bake for 6–8 minutes, until brown at the edges. Remove with a spatula to a rack to cool.
Makes 20–25

Mountain lakes in the Conor Pass

SODA BREAD WITH ONIONS

This variation on classic Irish soda bread is good with
potted meats and pâtés.

1 lb 2 oz/500 g strong
white flour
1 large onion, finely chopped
4 tablespoons olive oil
$^1/_2$ teaspoon salt
1 teaspoon bicarbonate
of soda
1 pint/575 ml buttermilk
2 teaspoons caraway seeds

Preheat the oven to
180°C/350°F/Gas Mark 4. Chop
the onion finely and cook them in
a heavy pan, in a tablespoon of
the oil, until dark brown and crisp
but not burned. Cool.

Sift the flour and salt together.
Dissolve the soda in a tablespoon
of buttermilk. Add this, with the
remaining 3 tablespoons of olive
oil, to the buttermilk. Add the
onions and seeds to the flour.
Make a well in the centre and
add the liquid. With a fork, mix it
all together thoroughly, mixing
lightly until you have a fairly
smooth texture. With floured
hands, shape the mixture into a
round cake, cut a cross in the top,
transfer to a greased baking sheet
and bake until the loaf gives a
hollow sound when tapped on
the bottom, about 40 minutes.

Note: if buttermilk is not
available, use fresh milk and
2 teaspoons of baking powder.

A film set from the film Far and Away, *Co. Kerry*
Overleaf: Garrettstown Strand, Courtmacsherry Bay, Co. Cork

QUEEN OF PUDDINGS

Here is a lighter version of this favourite, which pleases all ages.

5 eggs
$^3/_4$ pint/425 ml cream
$^1/_2$ pint/280 ml milk
a small piece of
  cinnamon stick
1 teaspoon grated lemon zest
1 teaspoon vanilla essence
2 tablespoons caster sugar,
  for the pudding
3 oz/75 g fresh breadcrumbs
4–5 tablespoons
  raspberry jam
6 oz/170 g caster sugar,
  for the meringue

Separate 3 of the eggs and set whites aside for meringue. Beat the remaining eggs and yolks together with the cream, milk, flavourings and 2 tablespoons of sugar. Put the breadcrumbs in an ovenproof dish, pour the cream mixture over them and infuse for several hours.

Preheat the oven to 170°C/325°F/Gas Mark 3 and bake for 15–20 minutes, until set. Allow to cool for a few minutes, then spread the jam over the surface.

Raise the heat to 190°C/375°F/Gas Mark 5. Beat the egg whites until they form stiff peaks. Sprinkle 3 oz/75 g of the sugar in slowly, whisking continuously, and then fold in the remaining sugar thoroughly. Spread the meringue over the jam completely and bake for 15 minutes until the meringue is set and brown, being careful it does not burn.

Serves 6

index